THE MURDER OF PRINCESS DIANA

THE MURDER OF PRINCESS DIANA

NOEL BOTHAM

PINNACLE BOOKS
KENSINGTON PUBLISHING CORP.
http://www.kensingtonbooks.com

To Lesley Lewis with my love for her constant support and encouragement with this investigation.

PROLOGUE

After the birth of Prince Harry, Princess Diana lived with the constant fear of being murdered. She regularly warned staff and friends not to be surprised should she suddenly turn up dead.

Despite all her warnings, virtually no one imagined that Diana's sudden, shocking death could be anything other than a tragic accident. Any lingering feelings of unease or vague suspicions about the cause of the crash were smothered by an overwhelming surge of anger, twenty-four hours later, when the French police and judiciary revealed that her driver, Henri Paul, was three times over the legal drink limit when he rammed the Mercedes into a concrete pillar. "As drunk as a pig" is how he was described, and there were traces of drugs in his blood to boot.

Newspapers around the world concluded—as they were intended to—that the culprit had been identified. A drink-sodden French chauffeur, ca-

reening along at 120 miles per hour, was the mon-
ster who had caused the death of the century's
best-loved woman.

This revelation—in my opinion, from the Paris
police—was a deliberate lie. It was created in panic
during a crisis meeting between senior French
government officials and the head of the Paris police, who had already had reports of MI6 involvement. This meeting took place after several hours
of urgent and frank talks between faceless figures
in London and Paris, and their brief was to identify a simple, acceptable solution for the crash, involving a single culprit. They were to label it,
categorically, an accident.

The Paris Criminal Brigade was put in charge of
the investigation. Its leader, Martine Monteil, a
smart and stylish fast-track career officer, had already learned that Henri Paul had worked not
only for MI6 but also for French Intelligence and
the French criminal investigation department *la
Sûreté*. She had also been told the driver had very
recently had a huge sum of money paid into his account, which could not be explained, and was carrying the equivalent of £2,000 in cash when he
died.

To the harassed police officer, under enormous
pressure from the Elysée Palace, Henri Paul must
have seemed the ideal scapegoat. The glaringly apparent relevance of his secondary income and his
connection with the intelligence services might be
downgraded if he were quickly and clearly established as the villain. She was encouraged by her su-
perior, Paris police commander Jean-Claude Mules.

Henri Paul was their guilty man and his private
life was unimportant. Monteil pursued this theory

rather than the seven paparazzi photographers, under arrest since the morning of the "accident," who had been accused of causing the crash by harassing the princess in a high-speed pursuit through the city. Bolstering this initial cover-up, Martine had already seriously discredited the first and subsequently important eyewitness. Eric Pètel would say that no photographers were following the Mercedes when it crashed. He had crawled into the back of the car alone and found the princess bleeding from her mouth and ear. The police discouraged press and television journalists from talking to this man. When he made his first report to the police, Pètel was switched to another part of Paris. They did not want him talking to the media.

In France it can be illegal for the authorities, both police and judicial, to reveal any information about an investigation until after a judge has concluded his inquiries and announced a verdict. Far from having reached a conclusion, the judge for this case had not even been appointed. Judge Hervé Stephan was only picked to head the inquiry twenty-four hours after the leak about Henri Paul's drinking. The truth is that at this stage, thirty hours after the crash, the alleged samples of Henri Paul's blood had not even been analyzed.

When the police did eventually come up with a blood sample which matched their claim of Paul being three times the legal drink limit, they discovered, to their extreme embarrassment, that this particular blood specimen also contained 20.7 percent carbon monoxide. This reading meant that apart from being the victim of crippling headaches and vomiting, the blood's owner would have been virtually incapable of either walking or driving.

I have been informed by a reliable source that on that same night in Paris there was another death to be investigated: a depressed character had downed a large quantity of alcohol before attaching a hose from the exhaust of his car to the interior. The sample of this man's blood, said my police informant at the pathology laboratory, would have had a similarly high percentage of carbon monoxide in it, a percentage equivalent to the sample purporting to be from Henri Paul. Even though the blood of this suicide case was analyzed in the same laboratory as that of the victims in Diana's car, no official checks were ever made as to there having been a mix-up in the blood samples or some kind of cross-contamination.

The police also refused then, and still refuse today, to identify any of the other twenty-two persons classified as "investigable deaths" who were dealt with that night, or to release the pathology results of tests on their blood. It is difficult to understand their refusal if they have nothing to hide.

The pathologists involved, backed by Martine Monteil of the Criminal Brigade and the prosecutor's office, also refused to allow independent samples to be taken from Paul's body, or to allow independent tests on the blood and urine samples alleged to have been taken from his body during the autopsy. No outside party, including Henri Paul's parents, was permitted to have a representative pathologist present when the body was reexamined or further samples taken of tissue or fluids. French judges have also refused to allow DNA tests to be carried out on the blood and urine samples which it was claimed came from Henri Paul's cadaver, and so no independent positive match has been attempted. Even had such tests been permitted, there could be no guarantee that the samples produced later were actually those which the French police claim were used to obtain the original results.

In these circumstances, it is impossible to accept without question that the body in question was indeed that of Henri Paul. It might have been anyone.

No serious investigator now accepts, for many reasons, that the blood samples referred to by the police were really those of Henri Paul, even though the French authorities will not admit what seems to have been either a mistake or a blatant substitution of samples.

Other equally serious cover-ups were made by the French police and judiciary, and details of information suppressed have come to light during the seven years since the crash. A photograph of the Mercedes, taken in close-up from the front in the Alma Tunnel where it crashed, and showing Diana and Dodi laughing happily just seconds before they died, is in the official judicial files—even though police swore such photographs did not exist. They claimed that the CCTV camera near the entrance to the tunnel was switched off that night. Other reports persisted for years that that camera, and others on the route, had been deliberately turned to direct them toward the side of the road. These have now been proved to have been part of the general cover-up. A motorist who had passed through the tunnel just minutes before the crash occurred received an automatic fixed-penalty speeding notice fifteen days later. It quoted evidence from the exact camera that the police claimed had been switched off. The Paris authorities appear to be fully aware that the camera had captured pictures of Diana's car and their lies were in danger of being exposed just weeks after the crash, but they made no public admission and have never corrected their original misleading statements. Only when the details of the speeding ticket were revealed, six years after the fateful night, did the truth become clear.

If this was a simple, straightforward accident, as they maintain, then why was it felt necessary to keep quiet about the camera? It makes no sense—unless it was part of a cover-up.

It is understood that at least one other photograph in the official judicial files—also shot through the windshield—came from another source. The police and the prosecutor's office refuse to discuss it.

Police also denied for three weeks the existence of a small white Fiat which witnesses claimed had swerved toward Diana's car moments before it crashed. When he did finally concede such a car might have been involved, police commander Jean-Claude Mules personally limited the search area for this car to two Parisian suburbs adjoining the tunnel where the crash occurred. When the car was discovered by independent investigators and found to have belonged to a French paparazzi photographer who had falsely denied being present in Paris on the night of the crash, the Criminal Brigade and its boss Martine Monteil apparently did not mention it to the judge. Mules told her to let it drop. He had personally interviewed the photographer, James Andanson, and declared him to be innocent of any crime.

Even after they identified this photographer as probably having worked for MI6 and other intelligence agencies, the police would still not admit he might have played a role in the accident. They claimed there was no match between his Fiat and paintwork found on the Mercedes, despite independent experts testifying that the paints were a perfect match.

Incredibly, Paris police and the investigative judge reacted mutely to the news that the photographer's charred body had later been found in the burned-out wreckage of his car, hundreds of miles from home and in very mysterious circumstances. The car was locked but the keys were missing. The man himself was supposed to have been in a completely different part of France at the time of his death. Even with these glaring anomalies, this too was not considered worthy of further investigation by the Criminal Brigade. Local officials are unhappy with the suicide verdict which was brought in because of the lack of any conflicting evidence, but say they are willing to reopen the case if fresh evidence can be produced. Certainly there is growing speculation that he might have been dispensed of to prevent him from revealing details of the Diana assassination plot.

Why was the Paris traffic police report on the accident not given to the investigating judge, and why was the tunnel road reopened just hours after the crash and cleaned with detergent before a detailed forensic search could be made and valuable evidence preserved?

These, and many other vital facts, will be examined in detail later in this book, and will show that the crash which caused the death of Princess Diana was no accident: she was deliberately killed.

Most of the evidence points toward the security forces being responsible for the assassination. But if they planned the actual operation, on whose orders were they acting? The British government, the Americans or the royals themselves?

Princess Diana herself was never in any doubt as to who her killers would be, though in fact there was more than one group with the motive and resources for the operation. Her main enemies, she was convinced, were her husband and a sinister hard core of palace watchdogs, each under secret oath to defend the royal family against intolerable events and scandals.

Diana lived constantly with the fear of being assassinated, and put her thoughts in writing just one year before her death. She believed she was the subject of comprehensive surveillance by an unseen enemy, her destiny and that of her children in the hands of lackeys and sycophants of her husband who had tarnished her as an unbalanced paranoid.

But she believed it was Prince Charles himself who was the greatest threat. She believed he wanted her dead.

In October 1996, she wrote, "This particular phase in my life is the most dangerous. My husband is planning 'an accident' in my car . . . brake failure and serious head injury in order to make the path clear for him to marry."

If Princess Diana believed this, and talked about

it, then others must have known—the kind of courtier, perhaps, who would believe he would be doing the prince a great service by ridding him of this detested woman whose death was the simple key to Charles's happiness.

The only survivor of the crash, bodyguard Trevor Rees-Jones, suffered horrendous injuries and has never been able to remember a single detail of the actual drive—though he recollects everything preceding it that night. His main fear is that his memory will return. "If I remember, they will kill me," he said. "Every single day I fear for my life."

What is there in his subconscious that is prompting such real fear in his conscious mind? Or has he already remembered what he saw in those last few moments before the crash, and will not admit to it because to do so would be like signing his own death warrant?

The less-than-loyal butler Paul Burrell also feared attempts on his life by "the dark forces at work in the country." There are those, he believes, who want to prevent him revealing further royal secrets which he claims pose an even greater threat to the future of the royal family than those already published.

Princess Diana's terror was so real that when she lost her HRH status after her divorce from Prince Charles, she refused a police personal protection squad despite considerable pressure from the palace. Isolated, vulnerable and believing herself to be constantly at risk, she was convinced an assassination attempt would almost certainly be made by the British security forces, which include the royal protection squad, made up of some of the very people she feared.

She had also been warned by diplomat friends in

Washington that she was a possible target for American security "laundrymen," whose clean-up technique involves the ultimate sanction of assassination. Many American politicians and law-enforcement officers believe that when President John F. Kennedy publicly committed himself, in the summer of 1963, to withdrawing every American serviceman from Vietnam by Christmas, it was tantamount to signing his own death warrant. Too many unscrupulous men were making too much money from the war to want it ended. Then, as now, there could be no profit in peace for men like these. His successor, Lyndon Johnson, proved it by sending a further 250,000 American troops to Vietnam.

Diana's highly successful campaign to outlaw the use of land mines and eventually force a cutback of all arms sales had, inevitably, brought her into direct conflict with the same very rich—and equally ruthless—manufacturers and salesmen of military hardware. They and the Pentagon launched a massive lobbying campaign to force the White House to maintain a land mines option.

The princess was clearly considered a powerful opponent by these international arms dealers and the military supremos at the Pentagon who supported them. This was effectively, and publicly, demonstrated when—to her opponents' joint dismay—she persuaded President Clinton to support a land mines treaty which would be signed by all the world's major powers. Already considered a loose cannon in some quarters, Diana was now confirmed as a real menace to certain major American industrialists who saw Clinton's commitment to the princess as a direct threat to their future arms profiteering. Enormous political pressure was put

on the president to renege on his promise to the
princess. At the same time, admit some within the
intelligence community, ways of silencing Diana,
or hijacking her campaign, also became subjects
for discussion.

Diana was killed just three weeks before the
Oslo conference of September 19, 1997, at which
Britain and most of the western world signed the
land mines treaty. The only western power which
refused to sign was the United States. Bill Clinton
had been convinced of the "advisability" of breaking his promise to the late princess. His reversal of
policy may well not have happened had she lived.
It was a risk these protagonists of war were not prepared to take.

The United States government archives in
Washington contain top-secret files on the activities of Princess Diana, totaling a staggering 1,190
pages. These files were assembled by the CIA, the
FBI and the National Security Agency (NSA) which,
among other undertakings, monitors sensitive telephone calls on a worldwide basis.

According to an intelligence source in Washington, the surveillance activity surrounding Princess
Diana increased dramatically after she became involved in the land mines appeal, and intensified
even more after President Clinton agreed to back
her. "At the same time, Pentagon and arms-industry
lobbying against a U.S. involvement in the treaty
became intensive. You don't get that much focus
from these guys unless they are planning to do something specific," he said.

The files may well have a bearing on the death
of Princess Diana, but the United States government has flatly refused to release any of the details

they contain. When, after her death, American newspaper editors called for the release of the security agencies' files on Diana, the State Department decreed that all 1,190 pages of documents must remain locked away indefinitely. The State Department spokesman, in justification, told the *New York Daily News*, and others, that revealing their contents would "seriously jeopardize the national security of the United States of America"!

American lawyers who want to know what the files contain are perplexed by the government's dramatic response. They understand the intelligence agencies could well feel embarrassed if it were to become known that they had spied on a member of the royal household of a friendly nation. What they do not understand is how files on the princess could endanger their country's security.

A former U.S. agent confirmed that orders came "from the very top" to spy on the princess and bug all the places she stayed during her frequent trips to America, and to keep her under constant, twenty-four-hour-a-day surveillance. He told me this was carried out with the full knowledge of British prime ministers John Major and Tony Blair, after they had been convinced that it was necessary to ensure the security of the royals. Monitoring of Diana's movements and telephone calls continued right up to the time of her death through the top-secret American surveillance center in Britain. The results were, under an agreement between the two countries' intelligence services, routinely passed on to MI5, MI6 and Special Branch. Likewise, pertinent British intelligence on the princess was given to their opposite numbers in Washington. The Government Communication Headquarters (GCHQ) and the NSA have been cooperating as partners ever since the Thatcher–Reagan *entente* of the eighties.

Diana did not know the names or nationalities of the agencies which spied on her, but she knew they were there and used to have a former "spook" regularly sweep her home for electronic bugs. She dubbed the people responsible for organizing the surveillance "the men in gray suits." These are the same men and women who see themselves as Charles's protectors, and who move against anyone who threatens his reputation or weakens his position as king-in-waiting; the people the royals are referring to when they talk of the "dark forces."

Almost from the time of her marriage, which had already been exposed to her as a sham, the princess had felt enmeshed in a web of deception and palace intrigue which she found all-pervading; but she knew that few, other than herself, were even aware of it. She was convinced that a deep malaise existed within the highest echelons of the royal family, but when she attempted to expose the dysfunctional nature of the family, her revelations were dismissed as paranoid rubbish. Since her death, the full accuracy of these allegations has been recognized.

The face of this beautiful, uniquely popular woman dominated the front pages of every newspaper and magazine in the world for two decades and she was, had they possessed the common sense to recognize it, the jewel in the crown of the British royal family. But they chose to see only the flaws.

Those close to her knew that the gem that was Diana was always in danger of shattering. It was in the crucible of her childhood that the flaws were first forged in the girl who was to marry the heir to the throne.

She loved her parents, yet her lasting memory of childhood was the clatter of her mother's high-heeled shoes on the marble staircase of their house in London's Belgravia, the sound of the front door slamming as her mother walked out on her father—without saying goodbye to her children. Diana was ten years old when her mother bolted from her own loveless marriage to Earl "Johnny" Spencer. It was a memory that haunted her for the rest of her life. Even though her mother came back for them, Diana told friends that she had spent the rest of the night weeping and trying to console her little brother who was too young to understand how the constant bickering of their parents had finally boiled over and scalded their happiness.

With the right husband—a man offering love, tenderness and affection—Diana might have overcome the trauma of her parents' breakup and her own insecurity, but Charles was unwilling, or simply unable—perhaps due to the effects of his own miserably unhappy childhood—to express genuine affection for this tragic young woman who was cuckolded even before she approached the altar. Charles and Camilla Shand had enjoyed a passionate and intense affair in the summer of 1972. It might have progressed had she not been judged by the royal family to be "secondhand goods": too many people knew of her relationship with Andrew Parker Bowles, and that she was not a virgin. That alone was enough to rule her out as a future Princess of Wales. It is significant that Charles should argue today that it does not rule her out as a future Queen.

Andrew, a friend of the young prince, had been Camilla's steady boyfriend since 1966, and there was an understanding between them that one day they would marry. But in 1969 Andrew didn't hesitate to cast her aside when the nineteen-year-old Princess Anne fell in love with the dashing cavalry officer and surrendered her virginity to him. Despite being the Queen Mother's godson—his father had been her closest male friend after the death of George VI—and a popular figure at court, Andrew was fully aware that there was no future in the relationship. The affair was passionate and intensely physical but Andrew knew that as he was a Roman Catholic it could never lead to marriage. He severed the relationship in 1972 and Anne was upset, but not heartbroken, by the end of the affair. She had already started seeing Captain Mark Phillips in 1971, and with classic Windsor morality was no more faithful to Andrew than he to her.

At the same time, Charles's torrid affair with Camilla was, regrettably for him, coming to an end. For Charles it had been a dizzying and overwhelming revelation—he had experienced satisfying, exciting and successful sex for the first time in his life—but they both knew that the mores prevailing at the time would rule out a permanent union. In addition, although she was extremely flattered to have her future king besotted by her—as Edward VII had been by her great-grandmother Alice Keppel, who was his mistress for twelve years until his death in 1910—Camilla was still in love with Andrew, and had already waited six years for her guards' wedding.

The following spring, Andrew proposed and Camilla accepted without hesitation. They married in July in the Guards Chapel in Birdcage Walk. Princess Anne was there, perhaps regretting what might have been. Charles, not present though perhaps also sharing her regrets, was serving aboard HMS *Minerva*, then stationed in the Caribbean.

Andrew and Camilla's son, Tom, was born in December 1974. Charles was his godfather.

To Camilla, never a woman to let a question of morals spoil her fun, there now appeared no good reason why her affair with Charles could not be rekindled—and he enthusiastically agreed. From that moment on, Charles's physical dependence on Camilla was absolute. It had him hanging about her skirt tails at Bolehyde Manor, the Parker Bowles country home, and Andrew soon grew used to finding the prince there when he returned from army duties in the evenings.

Potential fiancées came and went, but Charles really wanted nothing to do with them. He had already found the woman who satisfied all his needs. Approximately half the prince's relationships with girls remained unconsummated because he was so well taken care of in that area by Camilla. She had also become his greatest confidante, and he shared with her the most intimate details of his merry-go-round hunt for a bride—however unenthusiastically pursued. In 1977 he offered his hand to Anna Wallace, the beautiful twenty-five-year-old daughter of a Scottish landowner. After watching Charles dance all evening with Camilla at the Polo

Ball, thrown by Lord Vestey at his Stewell Park stately home in Gloucestershire, she told him, "Not even you can treat me like this, and you'll never get another chance." Lieutenant Colonel Andrew Parker Bowles might have to put up with the public humiliation, but Anna let it be known— very vocally—that she would not.

In 1980, when Andrew was serving in Rhodesia, *Private Eye*'s correspondent "Grovel" noted, "Andrew, 39, is married to a former (?) Prince Charles fancy, Camilla Shand, and if I should find the royal Aston Martin Volento outside the Parker Bowles mansion while the gallant colonel is on duty overseas, my duty will be clear."

By now the couple didn't care what people thought about the relationship, and Andrew's return to England certainly didn't stop Charles overruling the advice from both the palace and Foreign Office that he not take Camilla with him as his escort to the Zimbabwe independence celebration. Their affair was already out of control, and for the first time members of Charles's entourage heard the phrase "Mrs. Parker Bowles is a nonnegotiable item." If Charles wanted his Pompadour involved in the royal pomp, then that was the way it would have to be!

In Camilla's eyes, unlike those of most of the other women in his life, Charles was never found wanting. With the others he was never particularly noted for his bedroom skills and was voted disappointingly inadequate as a lover by those of his girlfriends who were willing to talk. "He is the least tactile man I have ever known," said one. Another could not remember him ever having caressed her—in or out of bed. "He made love to satisfy himself," she recalled with a grimace. "What you might call Australianesque!"

Few of his girlfriends had wanted to prolong a relationship even with the matchless reward of becoming Queen of England. Some girls did not even have the consolation of social contact with Charles. They were delivered, by aides, to his bedroom in the homes of his many chums, made love to with little tenderness or satisfaction on their part, and spirited away. "He had the equipment but didn't know how to use it," was the verdict of one disappointed bed companion.

That the prince was nevertheless very generously endowed by nature in this area was recorded during his teens by a *Daily Express* photographer. Charles, being schooled in sailing technique by Uffa Fox, was stretched far out over the side of a yacht when the kilt he was wearing was blown up around his head. Measurements made later in the *Daily Express* darkroom revealed Charles to have appropriately regal proportions beneath his kilt.

The genius of Mrs. Parker Bowles, some in their circle claim with admiration, is that having recognized the prince's sparse qualifications as a lover, she convinced him he was the greatest Lothario in the kingdom and she was grateful to pander to his every whim. It is a technique and piece of harmless cajolery that has been practiced by clever paramours with men of meager bedroom talent throughout the ages. She asks for nothing, gives everything and lets him know she feels fortunate to be blessed with his attention.

That attention, which she enjoys today, is perhaps more visible but certainly no greater than it was in 1980, and the influence she wields over the prince also remains unchanged from those pre-Diana days. It was Camilla who persuaded him of the need to marry—if for no other reason than to produce an heir. And when he stumbled across Diana Spencer, by accident, it seemed to the pair of them to be almost too good to be true.

The Prince of Wales's calculated stalking of Diana, cold-blooded as his pursuit of a deer across the Balmoral estate, was as wickedly selfish an example of exploitation of an innocent and trusting teenage girl as it is possible to imagine. That the plot was effectively hatched in the bed of his mistress made it even uglier.

It was already clear to many of their contemporaries who had watched the public humiliation of Andrew Parker Bowles as the prince and his concubine frantically kissed and groped one another on the dance floor throughout the prestigious Cirencester Polo Club Ball in 1979, that the pair would sacrifice anyone's feelings, together with their own honor and decency, on the altar of their mutual desire. Observers found it an unpleasant and disturbing spectacle. But the treatment they were to mete out to Diana over the next fifteen years made their tormenting of Andrew Parker Bowles appear no more than a little harmless fun in comparison.

For a young woman, starved of affection and longing to be loved by anyone, it really seemed like a fairy tale come true when the handsome prince—the world's most eligible bachelor who would one day be king and make her his queen—said he had fallen in love with her. It was, she told her friends, just too fabulous to be true. And she was right. From the very outset, this cold-hearted, self-centered and self-serving man—reciting the words supplied by his equally selfish paramour— courted Diana with deliberate lies.

King Richard III is generally considered the most heartless and villainous monarch in British history. Yet there is no doubt that even he would have bowed an admiring knee to the distant successor to his throne in recognition of Charles's pitiless, calculated and cold-blooded treatment of Lady Diana Spencer.

It is important, if one is to understand the intense bitterness which eventually existed between Charles and Diana, between their two households and among the courtiers as a whole, that one recognizes the appalling nature of Charles and Camilla's treatment of Diana, and that the princess was aware of their relationship even before her marriage. Only then can one appreciate the motivation behind the Princess of Wales's vendetta against Charles, her paranoia and her need for revenge against the whole family—conditions which made Diana's removal not merely a viable, but increasingly a desirable option in some royal quarters.

In the last decade of her life, Diana had permitted her sexual exploits to run riot: she had ten different lovers in as many years. After her separation and divorce from Charles, her behavior became more irresponsible and unpredictable as her need for revenge rather than justice became established. She deliberately sought ways to shock and distress the royal family and, in rapid succession, she took a married English lover and became heavily involved with two Pakistanis and an Egyptian. This, she was certain, would particularly upset Prince Philip whom she was convinced was a racist.

What is still undeniable is that when she was killed, Diana was planning to marry Dodi Fayed. the Egyptian playboy, film producer and son of Harrods boss Mohamed Al Fayed. Diana intended moving to California where they would make their main home. Key staff in London had already been alerted about the move to Dodi's £4.5 million villa. Whether or not the wedding would have finally taken place is uncertain—but it was undeniably her intention at the time of her death.

These facts alone would have provided sufficient reason for some people to get rid of the princess. There are those who could not stomach the future king's mother being married to a foreign non-Christian. Security chiefs, for example, were concerned that the future monarch would have to travel abroad to visit his mother.

Other people in palace circles were deeply concerned about Diana's existing relationship with her eldest son, and the long-term effect it would have on him. William was barely fifteen, but for some time Diana had been confiding in him as though he were already an adult. To show she was a "cool" mum, she apparently allowed him soft porn magazines, typical among boys of his age increasingly interested in sex. More importantly she had made him the reluctant recipient of her most bizarre confidences, which streamed uncensored from her tortured psyche and included details of her sexual activities with her various lovers.

William had the remarkable sensitivity to react

with cries for help on his mother's behalf, though these produced more condemnation for her use—and abuse—of William than sympathy for his mother. They viewed the mother–son relationship through darkly critical eyes, and calculated the damage being done to the future king.

As if further complications were needed, the medical assistant from University College Hospital, who helped prepare her body for embalming, believed Diana was pregnant at the time of her death. The baby would have been an illegitimate half-brother, or half-sister, for William and Harry, and his father would have been neither British-born nor Christian.

A bungled attempt to cover up a suspected pregnancy had taken place in Paris before Diana's body was flown back to England. Partial embalming was authorized by the St. James's Palace office. While admittedly the father of her two children, as it happens Charles was no longer Diana's next of kin and thus had no legal right to authorize such a medical interference. Because of their divorce he was in fact no longer related to her in any way.

Commander Mules confirmed in Paris that the embalming decision was made by a much higher authority than him before the body was released. Without the permission of her next of kin, the tissue removal and the changes brought about by the introduction of embalming fluids became criminal assault—though it is unlikely that even Scotland Yard would have the courage to press charges. In 2003 it was revealed that the Princess went into a London hospital, only days before her last trip with Dodi, to undergo a pregnancy scan.

Yet, in some quarters, even these unwelcome

revelations were not believed to compare in their effect with the disclosures contained in secret tapes and videos which formed part of the Diana testament. These recordings were part of the contents of a closely guarded mahogany box, assembled by Diana to provide her with "insurance" against the feared assassins. She called the contents of this box her "Crown Jewels," and kept them in a locked safe. After her death the box was claimed by her sister, Lady Sarah McCorquodale. The contents were still intact when she checked it.

But when the box reached the Spencer estate at Althorp, it was empty.

Missing were an inscribed signet ring given to her by her former lover Major James Hewitt, several handwritten letters from Hewitt and senior members of the royal family, some twenty videotapes which were recorded in Kensington Palace when she was at her lowest ebb and which are a terrifyingly frank account of her marriage told in agonizing detail, and a single cassette audiotape which was a recording of her interview with former royal valet George Smith.

Some of the videos also referred to the interviews she conducted with George Smith at his home in Kensington Palace in 1996 and at the Priory, a private clinic, during a time when he was receiving treatment at Prince Charles's expense. Diana recorded Smith's allegations of having been raped on two occasions by a royal aide. A secret palace inquiry found there was no foundation to the allegations.

It was police knowledge of Diana's tapes which eventually led to an official investigation in 2001. It was dropped when Smith refused to press charges.

Prince Charles had already spent £100,000 on legal fees in relation to this matter.

But Diana had also taped evidence from George Smith of a potentially far more damaging episode, allegedly witnessed by the valet. The police had been told of this, and they were searching for it when they burst into Burrell's home in a dawn raid in 2001.

It was this particular incident—in which Smith alleges he had discovered Prince Charles and a senior royal aide cuddled together and stark naked in bed—that courtiers described as a time bomb ticking under the throne.

This was a devastating accusation, and since 1996 senior royals and the courtiers who chose to support their continued existence, had been terrified of it becoming public knowledge.

Charles was on record as saying that it was only this aide whom he trusted to squeeze his toothpaste onto his brush. He had also, he said, allowed the aide to assist him in directing a urine sample into a bottle for medical tests.

This tape, Diana's traumatic account of her marriage, and reports of her secret relationship with the Queen's nephew, Viscount Linley, another huge skeleton rattling hard to come out of the royal family's closet and threaten further intense scandal, are the catastrophic revelations which the royal family believed must be prevented from leaking out at any cost, and are the real reasons why the Burrell trial had to be stopped. Viscount Linley denied any intimate relationship with Diana, saying that he and his cousin-in-law "were just good friends."

Prince Charles and the aide have both described George Smith's allegation as preposterous, and deny the incident ever took place. Certainly it is not alleged that any illegal act occurred.

Smith clearly remembers Diana "lapsing deeply into thought," rather than being distressed, by his recounting of this story. Her recordings, which contain her own account of how a palace cover-up was organized to hush up all Smith's allegations, coupled with other revelations about the royals and a handwritten letter from James Hewitt, made suppression of the contents of Diana's wooden box, if not in themselves a fully valid reason for having her killed, then in some quarters a good enough contributory reason for doing so.

It seems barely credible, in just eighteen years, that Diana could have metamorphosed from the unknown and extremely innocent teenager she was when Prince Charles first met her, to the woman—so worshipped and desired by so many, so hated and reviled by a very powerful few—she had become on the day of her murder in August 1997.

PART ONE

THE MARRIAGE

ONE

Those who know the couple well say that after Charles spotted Diana at a weekend house party in West Sussex, where they were fellow guests, he showed uncharacteristic excitement. Even Diana herself remembered, "He was all over me like a rash—almost leaped on me there and then." It was not the kind of princely behavior she had been warned to expect by her two sisters, Jane and Sarah, who, having themselves failed to "bag" the royal heir, had already groomed their baby sister for her turn, should the chance arise.

As it happened, Diana's feelings and intentions were irrelevant. Charles had discovered a candidate for matrimony who fulfilled all the criteria defined by Camilla Parker Bowles, and it was this that had prompted his enthusiasm.

Diana turned down his invitation to drive her back to London—another tip from her sisters was not to be too compliant—and Charles returned to

Buckingham Palace alone, from where he telephoned his mistress to report his "find." Lady Diana Spencer, he told her, had all the wifely attributes they were seeking: she was a virgin without a past, and came from good, blue-blooded breeding stock.

Mrs. Parker Bowles immediately set about stage-managing the royal suitor's next moves in the wooing of their chosen bride. After a night of Verdi at the Albert Hall, Diana was invited to Cowes week aboard the royal yacht *Britannia,* and the cruise to Scotland which traditionally followed. This trip and the following spell in Balmoral was the testing period with the royal family: Diana passed with flying colors. Even Prince Philip, who had despaired of his eldest son ever taking a wife, was fulsome in his approval. "She can provide the family with some height," he commented—putting her about on a par with a brood mare. Yet this parental approval, though important, was insignificant to Charles compared with the real test.

Mrs. Parker Bowles and her husband were part of the Balmoral house party, and this would be Camilla's first chance to vet Diana in person. Her judgment, a rare miscalculation for Camilla, was that Diana was a mouse: ideal wife fodder who was incapable of breaking her stranglehold on the prince.

Cheered by Camilla's overwhelmingly favorable verdict, Charles sent Diana packing back to London escorted by, of all people, Andrew Parker Bowles, while he and his mistress—with typical lack of discretion—got on with their love affair.

During this wooing period, Diana had to put up with weekend after weekend at Bolehyde as a guest of the Parker Bowleses and with Camilla's never-ending advice to her on how best to get along with Charles. She learned that it was Camilla who had helped Charles choose Highgrove, a nine-bedroom Georgian mansion set in 350 acres, which was small for the heir to the throne but perfect for the prince's immediate needs. It was just a few minutes drive from the Parker Bowles house—and the woman with whom he had become totally besotted. It was Camilla, too, who had advised on its decoration. When Charles took Diana to the races, the chaperone he chose to be with them was Mrs. Parker Bowles. And it was to Camilla's home that they returned afterward—not Highgrove.

Diana was not the brightest girl in her class, but even she was capable, before long, of recognizing what was going on between her suitor and his friend's wife. Despite this, she still had dreams of her own to fulfill, paramount being her vision of becoming Queen of England. So she said nothing and prayed that the affair would not become as obvious to the general public as it was to her. It is quite unforgivable that, at this stage, her mother, who knew exactly what the relationship was between Charles and Camilla, did not warn Diana off. She urged caution, as any mother might have done, but despite knowing everything she said nothing that really counted.

Diana's grandmother, Lady Fermoy, was more to the point. "I don't think marrying into the royal family will suit you," she told Diana. "Their sense of humor and their lifestyle are very different." But by then it was already too late to protect her. Diana had been made painfully aware, courtesy of the *Sunday Mirror* on November 16, 1980, that her boyfriend—her first ever boyfriend—was sleeping with another woman.

The *Sunday Mirror* exclusive was that on the night after attending Princess Margaret's party at the Ritz Hotel with Charles, Diana had slipped down to Staverton in Wiltshire, where the prince had been entertaining Duchy of Cornwall officials, and sneaked aboard the royal train which was parked overnight in a siding. She and Charles, it suggested, had secretly spent the night together as lovers.

Six people knew for certain the story was untrue: Diana and her three flatmates who were in their Chelsea apartment watching television; Charles, who, the official train telephone log showed, had made a late-night call to the Parker Bowles home—and Camilla, the blonde-haired woman in the *Sunday Mirror* story, who had immediately dashed across country to be with her lover.

Charles displayed his fury to the *Sunday Mirror* and its then editor, Bob Edwards, and ordered the palace press secretary, Michael Shea, to denounce the story as a complete fabrication. This deliberate lie, not the first and certainly not the last he would tell about his relationship with Camilla, was hardly the conduct to be expected from a future king.

Diana, anxious not to be labeled a hussy, but stopping short of revealing the mystery blonde's real identity—of which she had no doubts at all—for the first time telephoned a royal correspondent, James Whitaker of the *Daily Mirror*, and told him, "It isn't true. I stayed in all night with my friends. We never left the flat. Believe me. I am not a liar."

At Charles's insistence a complaint was made to

the Press Council, but the palace press office—
made aware by the security services of the real
facts—said they would not proceed with the matter.

The one man to suffer from the deception was
Bob Edwards, a decent editor whose integrity and
judgment had been seriously undermined by the
prince's actions. It was months before he learned
the truth and six years before the palace "apologized" by awarding him a CBE (Commander of
the Order of the British Empire) for outstanding
services to journalism.

Diana never did receive an explanation from
the prince. In fact she didn't see Charles again for
several weeks. On New Year's Day 1981 she was invited to Sandringham. Had she expected his proposal at the Queen's Norfolk home then she was
to be disappointed. Despite Prince Philip's obvious frustration at his son's reluctance to take his
growled advice—"For God's sake, bloody well get
on with it"—Charles let the moment pass by. He already had a most enviable lifestyle and the perfect
mistress, so why change things?

It was only at Camilla's urging that the reluctant
prince unenthusiastically agreed to propose on his
return from a skiing trip in February. But it was not
until three days after his return from the ski slopes
of Klosters that Charles finally sent for Diana.

He had chosen Windsor Castle as the best setting, historically, for his proposal. Considering the
purpose of the meeting, it was arranged in a rather
old-fashioned, heavy-handed, master-to-servant fashion. The order to attend was not presented as an
invitation, Diana recalled later. "It was a royal command." And what should have been a joyous occasion was made tense and unnatural by Prince

Charles's inability to relax. He was stiffly formal throughout, she remembered, and did not kiss her or hug her or acknowledge her arrival with a touch of any kind. He asked her so suddenly, "Will you marry me?" that she burst out laughing.

"Yeah, OK," she replied, still giggling—not completely sure that it wasn't all some bizarre kind of joke.

Charles was not laughing. "You do realize that one day you will be queen?" he rebuked her.

"Yes," she said again, this time more meekly and not laughing at all.

It seemed enough for Charles, and he went straight off to another room in the castle to telephone his mother with the news. Diana was not required to speak to her future mother-in-law. To the prince it was "done and dusted," and he made no attempt to speak to her again for some time, even when she flew off to Australia to "get her breath back" and come to terms with the dramatically altered direction her life was about to take.

When, after a week of not hearing from him, and in desperation to speak to the man she thought loved her, Diana called Buckingham Palace, she was told he couldn't be found. He briefly returned her call the following day.

On her return to England she was welcomed home not by Charles but by one of his aides bearing flowers. She was left pretty much to her own devices until February 28, 1981, the day of the formal announcement of the engagement.

Their awkwardness, almost shyness, as they stood together before the TV cameras and the press for the first time could be best explained not by nerves but by the fact that they were each, publicly, making a lifetime's commitment to an almost complete stranger with whom they had virtually nothing in common. When the Prince of Wales was asked "Are you in love?," he could only manage a stammered, "Whatever 'in love' means" in reply. The feeble answer returned a thousand times or more to torment Diana during the next few months, and for the whole of her marriage.

After the press conference, Diana found herself bundled off to Clarence House, the Queen Mother's residence a few hundred yards from Buckingham Palace, where a suite of rooms had been made available for her. No member of the royal family, nor any of her friends, was there to offer support or reassurance; she had only learned of the move herself that morning. There was, however, one letter waiting for her, which had been written days earlier. It was from Camilla, who had known, well in advance, exactly where she would be staying, and it contained an invitation to lunch. If Diana had thought public recognition of her engagement to Charles would cool the ardor of the lovers and force an end to Camilla's participation in both their lives, she realized then that she was very much mistaken.

Shortly after this, Charles flew to Australia for a five-week royal tour. His farewell to Diana at Heathrow Airport was short and lacking in intimacy on his part, though she shed some tears. It was in marked contrast to the display of passion Charles had exhibited in Buckingham Palace a few hours earlier when Camilla had called to say goodbye. Diana had been with him in his office when the call came in, and had been forced to endure a gushingly sentimental farewell to his mistress which the prince had made no effort to disguise. It had left her angry, humiliated and tearful—and no doubt provided the real reason for those tears at the airport. It was a foretaste, Diana feared, of what life with Charles was going to become. It ripped apart her confidence and made her seriously question his real feelings for her.

Between then and the wedding very little happened to make her think differently. In the weeks after Charles returned from Australia he probably saw more of Camilla than he did of his fiancée— and the effect of this on Diana was punitive. The first real and visible manifestation of this newly created stress was the onset of bulimia. She had, by this time, moved into Buckingham Palace, with rooms close to the old nursery kitchen. There, several times a day, and often at night, she would have gorging sessions, wolfing down huge portions of rich food. These would be immediately followed by vomiting bouts in her private lavatory.

The servants who witnessed her binges and cleaned up her mess said nothing, and, as nobody in the palace apart from them knew what was happening to the desperately unhappy teenager, neither did anyone else.

The only two people having any doubts at all about the wisdom of what they were doing were the couple themselves. Both were having serious misgivings about the wisdom of going through with the marriage. Charles admitted to himself, only at this very late stage, that he shared not a single interest with this very young, very naive girl— and that at times he could barely tolerate being with her.

For her part, Diana had concluded that she was

worthless as a wife for the prince. Why else would her fiancé prefer to make love to an overweight, rather plain middle-aged housewife?

Correctly recognizing the catastrophe which lay ahead if the marriage were permitted to take place, Charles went to his parents and expressed his doubts. Prince Philip became so angry and abusive that his eldest son fled the room in terror. Looking for sympathy and solace, Charles next turned to Camilla for comfort. He was horrified when her reaction was equally as violent as that of his father. She knew far better than the prince what was good for him, she lectured. Didn't he trust her to do the right thing for him? Camilla refused to speak to him again until he came to his senses.

Diana fared no better.

Just three weeks before the wedding, and almost as a belated twentieth birthday party for Diana, the royals held a formal, white-tie-and-tails banquet at Windsor Castle where the thousand guests were entertained by Elton John. As a clear sign of things to come, Charles did not dance once with Diana, and went to bed early. She danced crazily in the disco until five in the morning, long after the other guests and even the servants had gone home. Then she drove home to her father at Althorp and told him that the wedding was off.

It would certainly have been more to his credit, and a far more fatherly gesture, had Earl Spencer heeded his youngest daughter's cry for help, put her happiness first, and called the whole thing off on Diana's behalf. Instead he spent the weekend convincing her that everything would be alright, that she was doing the right thing, and that it was her duty as a Spencer to return to London and fulfill her destiny.

Back at Buckingham Palace, where no comment was made by anyone concerning her runaway weekend, Diana invited her sisters to lunch and, just two days before her wedding day, begged for their support in calling it off. Believing her to be exhibiting simple, and very normal, pre-nuptial nerves, they were flippant, but adamant. "Your face is on the tea towels, it's too late to chicken out now." Jane and Sarah advised Diana that, in the end, Charles would not let her down.

They could not have been more appallingly wrong, as Charles himself confirmed five days before the wedding when he visited Broadlands and told Lord Mountbatten's grandson, Lord Romsey, that Camilla Parker Bowles was the only woman he had ever loved. "I could never feel the same way about Diana as I feel about Camilla," he confessed.

Desperately wanting to believe her sisters, Diana, not for the first time and certainly not for the last, put on a brave smile and that night looked radiant standing alongside the Prince of Wales at the head of the grand staircase in Buckingham Palace to receive eight hundred guests at a ball. Nancy Reagan was a guest of honor. Another honored guest, who shared the vintage Krug champagne and was entertained by the then popular group Hot Chocolate, was Mrs. Camilla Parker Bowles. Diana was determined not to allow her rival to spoil her evening, and was still smiling when she left in the early hours to Clarence House where she would spend her last day as a single woman.

For his part, Charles had no intention of remaining a single man that night. He returned to his suite in Buckingham Palace with Camilla, and they spent the rest of that night, according to his valet, making love. It was a staggering betrayal—not just of his bride, which was reprehensible, but of the Queen, the Church, the Archbishop of Canterbury (who would be officiating at his marriage to Diana in a little over twenty-four hours) and the whole nation, who genuinely believed he was giving himself, in all honesty and in the name of true love, to Lady Diana Spencer.

It would be many years before Diana found out about Charles's last, perfidious piece of treachery as a bachelor, but its effect on her was no less painful, the betrayal no less callous. Perhaps the princess felt some satisfaction at having had Camilla's name removed from the list of palace guests at the celebratory breakfast which followed their actual wedding—but it was pitiful revenge for such sickening behavior on the part of Charles and his mistress.

TWO

"There were three of us in this marriage, so it was a bit crowded."

Princess Diana's unforgettable declaration to Martin Bashir during the *Panorama* television interview in November 1995 was deliberately intended to throw Camilla Parker Bowles into the public spotlight, and in so doing make her public enemy number one. In both respects it succeeded, demonizing Camilla and, in the process, making Prince Charles the unquestionable villain of the royal marriage collapse.

It also prompted the queen to order their immediate divorce.

Diana did not escape the fallout unscathed. Supporters of Charles labeled her a woman in the advanced stages of paranoia, increasingly unstable and suffering from mental illness. But of far more importance to her was that she had made the first move to avenge fifteen years of almost uninterrupted despair and depression—loneliness and misery created uncaringly by her husband and his mistress. Not even the swearing of the sacred vows, made before God and the people during their marriage service in return for the blessing on their union from the Archbishop of Canterbury, had prevented Charles from taking Camilla with them on their honeymoon.

The newlywed Waleses were barely into their second day aboard the royal yacht *Britannia*, which they had joined at Gibraltar, when they had their first confrontation. Inevitably it concerned Camilla. Prized photographs of his paramour, which Charles kept in his diary, had fallen out while he was discussing his itinerary with Diana, and when she challenged him to give his reasons for carrying them, he refused even to discuss his friendship with Camilla. It ended in Diana going to bed in tears and Charles sleeping alone.

Diana blamed this incident for triggering a fresh outbreak of bulimia nervosa—her worst to date. She found herself frantically stuffing herself to capacity four or five times a day before inducing vomiting only minutes later. Far from attempting to comfort her and provide the simple reassurance that she held a special place in his affections, Charles's almost sadistic reaction was again to emphasize Camilla's importance to him by wearing her gift of a pair of gold cufflinks, each in the form of interlinked Cs—unsubtle reminders of the powerful and exclusive bond between them.

Had the marriage not by then been consummated—itself an unmemorable event, she recalled later—she would have refused him the questionable pleasure of exercising his marital rights. She told Andrew Morton, years later, "He was the man I wanted to be with for the rest of my life, and I was willing to jump through any hoop and over any hurdle to win him." But she was not prepared to be his second choice within her own marriage.

After their trying Mediterranean cruise they flew to Balmoral to continue a honeymoon that had become as idyllic as an endurance test, two strangers locked in a masquerade of intimacy. The situation would have been glaringly obvious to any other family in the land, but went completely unnoticed by Prince Philip, the Queen and the other members of the royal family on holiday there. The firm family rule on emotion was to "lock it in." No one was ever supposed to know what any of them was really feeling. "As the latest member of the family I would have been ignored anyway," Diana herself recalled. "Nothing I had to say was worth listening to."

After ten weeks of marriage, Diana was a changed person. Her waist was by now more than seven inches smaller than on the day her engagement had been announced, and she had lost so much weight she resembled little more than skin and bones. Her constant jealousy of Camilla, physically absent but permanently, it appeared to Diana, standing between herself and her husband, was the cause of endless fights and her ever-worsening bulimia. The illness sapped her strength and confidence, and she was barely able to speak to other members of the family, but amazingly no one but Charles even seemed to notice. More amazing still, from Diana's point of view, was that she found herself just as much in love with her prince as at the outset.

The public had never doubted it. They believed

wholeheartedly in the fairy-tale aspect of the romance and marriage, exactly as it had been presented in the press, and their demand for fresh information about the new Princess of Wales was unprecedented. Bewildered newspaper editors, faced with the daily call for more pictures and stories, were starting to accept that Dianamania was here to stay.

All that was required to make reality match the public illusion and turn the marriage into a brilliant success was an injection of romance from Charles, and a frank admission from him that Camilla had been dumped for good. Tragically for them both, and for a nation of well-wishers, Charles was emotionally too miserly to make the effort. Diana had to make do with his hurtful indifference and his heartbreaking but categorical refusal to end his relationship with Camilla.

The princess's private secretary, Patrick Jephson, was later to conclude that her approach to love had been conditioned by long-suppressed traumas in her early life. They had permanently damaged her ability to give or receive love. Suicidal because of her desperate need for help, confused by the contrast between Charles's callous insensitivity and the public's deification of her, an extremely unhappy Diana flew to London early in October to seek professional counseling. The doctors and psychologists who were called to examine her at Buckingham Palace diagnosed various tranquilizers to stabilize her condition. Diana refused to take any of them. She did not need drugs, she told them. She needed time alone with her husband to work things out, and she needed regular affection. The doctors insisted but Diana refused.

It was an impasse only broken when the princess discovered she was pregnant. Long before his birth she had something to thank William for, she would remark years later. With her condition confirmed, there was no question of her taking drugs, Diana told the doctors triumphantly. They might harm her unborn baby—possibly their future king.

Being pregnant produced an immediate surge of hope and optimism in the princess, who truly believed it would provide the elusive catalyst which would inject the missing spark into her marriage. But, as on most other occasions when she hoped her marriage would take a turn for the better, she was to be bitterly disappointed.

Having survived the honeymoon and the temper tantrums of the woman he now compared to an alien being, Charles was also in need of a reassuring cuddle and the unrestrained and undemanding affection of someone who loved him unreservedly. Only one woman could fulfil these needs for Charles: Camilla Parker Bowles.

Thus, on November 2, 1981, three days before the world learned that his wife was expecting their first child, Charles was back in the arms of his mistress, with whom he had secretly arranged a rendezvous during the meet of the Vale of the White Horse Hunt near Cirencester. It was never a real contest: Camilla's voluptuous curves versus Diana's skeletal form; the passionate, sexually arousing grown-up woman versus the bashfully uncertain, naive, sexually unskilled ingénue. After four months in denial, Charles was again in the secure embrace of his one great love—and he determined never to be separated from her again.

Diana did not discover that Charles had renewed his adulterous relationship with Camilla for another eight months, after the birth of Prince William in June 1982, but she seemed to know, instinctively, that he was being unfaithful, and constantly accused him, even without evidence, of betraying her.

After one particularly vocal and unpleasant row at Sandringham where they were celebrating their first New Year as a married couple, Diana, now three months pregnant and suffering the most appalling morning sickness, was heard to scream that she intended to kill herself. When Charles called her bluff, she hurled herself down a shallow flight of wooden stairs, landing in a bundle at the bottom, where she was found by a horrified Queen Mother. Incredibly, even though a local doctor and Diana's gynecologist had been urgently summoned, Charles simply walked away from his bruised and sobbing wife and went riding. It was to become his pattern of behavior for similar future incidents, of which there were to be several.

These "suicide bids" occurred over the next few years. They were never serious attempts to take her own life, but were rather cries for help from an increasingly desperate and isolated young woman. They were cries that went unheeded because Charles refused to take them seriously. He treated each attempt with either scorn or indifference, or a mixture of the two, even though on one occasion she slashed her wrists with a razor blade and on another cut her breast and thighs with a penknife, drawing blood. He simply chose to ignore her, as he did when she made enormous efforts to do the right thing in public. She told a friend that she was trying so damn hard and all she needed was a pat on the back, like a dutiful horse. But it was not forthcoming.

It was immensely stressful for such a naturally shy person as Diana to thrust herself onto the center stage, and if Charles seemed oblivious to the pains she was taking over her royal duties, Diana soon recognized, with growing satisfaction, that the public more than appreciated her efforts. It soon became apparent that it was her, and not Charles, whom the crowds had turned out to see.

After William's birth, which briefly gave them one joint achievement they could celebrate together, the couple were rarely in accord, and less than a year after their wedding the royal couple found their marriage inexorably disintegrating. Postnatal depression and a new outbreak of bulimia had Diana in their grip and were eroding what few reserves of strength she had left. Perversely, what little energy remained to her she used to attack her husband, whom she had finally caught declaring his everlasting love for Camilla in a late-night telephone call from his bath. They had stopped sharing their four-poster marital bed even before William was born, and Charles slept in the spare bed in his dressing room. The staff knew this to be true because the prince's threadbare Teddy now lived there when he was in Highgrove—Teddy was his companion everywhere he went, as housekeeper Wendy Berry remembered. The only person who was allowed to repair the ancient, patched-up cuddly toy was Charles's nanny, Mabel Anderson.

Diana's spirits briefly rallied after Andrew Parker Bowles was promoted to commanding officer of the Household Cavalry, and she learned that the Parker Bowleses were moving; but they sank as quickly when they bought Middlewick House near Corsham, even closer to Highgrove than before, and Charles became a frequent traveler along the twelve miles of roads separating the two homes.

His conjugal life with Diana was not quite over, however. She had given him an heir, but to be safe he still needed "a spare," as Diana was later to describe their second-born. But after Harry was born in September 1984, the royal couple ceased making love together. Charles's affair with Camilla Parker Bowles continued to be the major cause of their frequent, stormy confrontations, but although getting rid of Camilla was a very tall order for Diana, another task she was determined not to shirk was her planned purge of the Prince of Wales's "Pink Mafia," as she had dubbed his predominantly homosexual staff.

Lord Mountbatten, known affectionately around the palace as the biggest queen in the royal family, had surrounded Charles with homosexuals during the period when he had been entrusted by Queen Elizabeth with her eldest son's social upbringing. Diana did not like the clique that was similarly intended to be around her two sons and had systematically got rid of over forty gay members of her husband's staff by forcing resignations or personally firing them. She may have then had a reactionary hostility toward homosexuality that was later to transform in maturity to the affection for some gay men and her public support for HIV victims, but whatever the reason, the prince's aides feared her and her legendary hot temper.

Diana in a fury became a screaming, door-slamming, foot-stamping harridan. Charles was determinedly and infuriatingly nonconfrontational. He would refuse to answer her questions or respond to her accusations, just turning his back and walking away from the fracas, leaving Diana even more spitting mad. "Above all else, she hated to be ignored," said her former private secretary Patrick Jephson.

Wendy Berry, their Highgrove housekeeper, remembered, "The prince's indifference would have been crushing for anyone. He was so aloof and uncaring. I began to see the absolute desperation and frustration felt by both the prince and the princess, having to live within a marriage that was patently falling apart at the seams."

During their most blistering rows they didn't care who heard them—even the children—and their language was straight from the gutter. Not for the first time the Highgrove staff watched as Prince Charles stormed out of the front door, jumped into his car and roared away down the drive. Diana was left at an open window screaming, "You're a shit, Charles, an absolute shit."

On another occasion she threw a teapot at him and marched away yelling, "You're a fucking animal, Charles, and I hate you."

Once, when she had answered him back with an expletive, he threw a wooden bootjack at her and shouted, "How dare you speak to me like that? Do you know who I am?" At times like this he could scarcely contain himself. American author Kitty Kelly reported that after one difficult exchange he stalked out of the room, strode into the bathroom, ripped the porcelain hand basin from the wall and smashed it on the floor. "You do understand, don't you? Don't you?" he asked his wide-eyed valet. Ken Stronach simply nodded.

It both baffled and angered Charles that this sick, unstable and remarkably unsophisticated woman—which is what he truly considered her to be—could be the object of such universal public adulation. With seemingly so little effort she could manipulate the crowds who were to be his, and not her, future subjects. The public and press were aware only of Diana—they wanted only *her* photograph, *her* reaction and *her* attention. In three years she had single-handedly resurrected the Windsors' tarnished image and virtually nonexistent popularity, and yet the royal family offered her nothing in return but their criticism—and secretly their envy.

Jealousy and resentment of her phenomenal success as the principal royal attraction already colored Charles's attitude toward Diana, and it began to affect him in other ways too, principally his growing dependence on Camilla who was his only true confidante on the subject of Diana and the only one capable of restoring his battered ego when the public repeatedly rejected him in favor of the princess. Charles's resentment was shared by several of his aides and other royal courtiers at Buckingham Palace, who were beginning to realize that Princess Diana could be a much greater threat to the stability of the royal family than anyone had so far realized.

It was in 1986, led, as often happened, by *Daily Mirror* royal correspondent James Whittaker, that the press finally became concerned about Diana's wasting figure. This grew more pronounced when she collapsed during the opening of Expo '86 in Vancouver. Charles wasn't entirely certain that it wasn't just another deliberate stunt to upstage him and grab the headlines. She had, after all, taken to outshining all the members of the royal family intentionally, even the Queen. At the state opening of parliament she turned out with her hair done up in a chignon which, as she intended, focused every scrap of attention, not to mention the press cameras, in her direction and away from the Queen. It made Elizabeth look a complete fool, as her irate sister, Princess Margaret, pointed out. The family was angered, but not overly concerned, at this demonstration of Diana's ability to manipulate the media. After all, wasn't she one of them? But it was already giving certain courtiers considerable cause to reevaluate.

What neither Charles nor the other observers at court had considered was that Diana might finally react to his adultery by taking a lover of her own.

The opportunity for her to do so had been there for the taking for almost a year. Royal Protection Squad Sergeant Barry Mannakee, a handsome thirty-seven-year-old, had become her official minder in 1985 and had quickly developed a special rapport with the princess. Soon afterward, at her suggestion, he was given the vital role of guarding Prince William, and became a firm favorite of the toddler.

Mannakee was married with two children and had seventeen years' experience as a police officer when he met Diana. His maturity impressed her and in just a few weeks he had become her closest confidante and friend. "She trusted him implicitly," said a former colleague, "and felt free to pour out all her woes to him. He became the recipient, or dumping ground might be a better term, for four years of stored up emotions and resentments. Until he came along, there was nobody she dared talk to."

Diana was aware of the scandal involving Royal Protection Squad Sergeant Peter Cross and the Princess Royal, and had sympathized when Anne began an affair with Cross after her marriage to Mark Phillips collapsed. Cross had been transferred to other duties when his relationship with Princess Anne became obvious.

Diana told her biographer Andrew Morton that she reserved her fondest memories for Barry Mannakee, who became her bodyguard at a time when she felt lost and alone in the royal world. Wrote Morton, "He sensed her bewilderment and became a shoulder for her to lean on and sometimes to cry on during this painful period."

For a woman with no self-worth or self-esteem, a trusted confidante like Mannakee was of enormous value. He was content to listen to her for hours on end, accompanying her on shopping trips or being at her side for long drives around the Balmoral estate when Charles disappeared on fishing expeditions. They grew very close. It was Barry, the son of working-class London parents, to whom Diana turned when she was unhappy or depressed. And it was Barry who would hug her when she was crying, and give her the reassurance she needed. Observers at the time believe it would only have taken a very small step for them to have become lovers. But despite various rumors and reports to the contrary, and a lurid account of a romance in at least one royal biography, their relationship did not become a physical one—although there were those in the palace who definitely believed otherwise.

Their friendship was terminated abruptly after Charles overheard Diana recounting details to Mannakee of the prince's own affair with Camilla, and listened to the policeman counsel her on how best she should deal with it. The furious prince telephoned a senior officer in the Royal Protection Squad and ordered Mannakee's immediate transfer from royal duties. There were several senior officers in the squad who resented Mannakee's easy closeness to the future queen—after all, he was a mere sergeant—and were pleased to see him switched to the Diplomatic Protection Corps.

A friend at the time said that Diana was stunned by the suddenness of the transfer. "He was about the only one she could talk to at that time. It was quite natural that they should become such close friends. This really hit her very badly. It was frightening for her to see the power other people had to so dramatically affect her life."

It was in 1985, I was told, that the British security services, in the shape of MI5 and Special Branch, embarked on the operation to bug all royal telephones and certain royal rooms. Ostensibly, it was said, the operation was launched purely to improve protection of the royals themselves; their personal conversations would not be stored or transcribed or passed to other intelligence organizations. In truth, after the Cross and Mannakee incidents, it was believed by the authorities that they could no longer rely on protection-squad officers to apprise them fully of what was happening with their charges. They were confident the new surveillance techniques would not intrude on the royals. Why should they? The royals were not told for many years that the new operation was even in place.

Perhaps because of her feeling of isolation at that time, Diana already suspected she was being spied upon, and blamed her husband and faceless palace courtiers. But in May 1987 she received the devastating news that Barry Mannakee had been killed in a road accident.

The news was broken to her by Prince Charles in a deliberately brutal and calculated way, designed to cause her the maximum of pain. A car was about to drop them on the airport tarmac for a royal flight to Cannes to attend the film festival. "Oh, by the way", said Charles, "I got news from the protection unit yesterday that poor Barry Mannakee was killed. Some sort of motorcycle accident. Terrible shame, isn't it?"

As the car stopped, Diana burst into tears. Charles pushed her out. "Let's go, darling," he said sarcastically. "Your press awaits you!"

Mannakee was a pillion passenger on a motorcycle being driven by a fellow police officer, Stephen Peat, which had collided with a car. Sergeant Mannakee died instantly. Peat suffered serious head injuries. Diana was convinced, from the moment she received the news, that Mannakee was the victim of an MI5 plot. "He knew too much about Charles and Camilla and what was going on," she said. Even when she was told that a seventeen-year-old girl, Nicola Chopp, had been charged with driving without due care and attention, she refused to believe his death was the result of a simple accident.

"They have all sorts of ways of arranging these things," Diana later told her lover Major James Hewitt. She confided in Hewitt that Barry Mannakee had been killed because they had developed too close a relationship and because she had told him too much about Prince Charles's affair with Camilla. "MI5 and the people at the palace killed him. I am certain they killed him. One day it will be me they come for."

"She maintained that belief the whole time I knew her," revealed Hewitt. "She was also fearful for my safety, for at that time she wanted to leave Charles so we could marry. 'You could be in danger,' she warned me, and hinted that someone might want to kill me too. We found two phone taps in Devon, where Diana and I stayed in my mother's home, and I am sure they were aware of most of my conversations and meetings with the princess. I was often followed and sometimes we noticed an observer when we met.

"I received two direct threats on my life—both from someone I knew. He said it was in the best interests of my health if I ended my relationship with Diana. Or I could meet the same end as Barry Mannakee. Warnings to back off also came from a member of the royal family and Diana's private secretary, Patrick Jephson."

The strength of Diana's feelings for Barry Mannakee can be judged by the annual pilgrimage she made to the crematorium where his ashes are scattered. She even made attempts to contact him through a medium.

A former senior intelligence officer confirmed that Mannakee's death could have been arranged, even though only one other vehicle seemed to be involved and a driver had been charged with an offense. "This type of fatal accident is not difficult to set up," he said. "Clearly other people would have to be involved but witnesses, if there were any, would not necessarily remember seeing them."

Diana certainly believed it had been stage-managed, and she blamed herself. "He died because of what he heard from me," she told Major Hewitt.

The princess believed that given the morals of today's royals it was a regular occurrence for the security services to have to clean up after some of their more bizarre romantic attachments. With her privileged vantage point right at the center of the royal family, Diana was in a position to know all of their secrets.

One of the earliest of the royal sex secrets, which ran in parallel to Prince Charles's adultery, concerned her outwardly staid sister-in-law the Princess Royal. Diana was fascinated, but hardly surprised, to discover that Anne's partner in adultery at the time Barry Mannakee was being transferred for "overfamiliarity" was Andrew Parker Bowles. Brother and sister—Charles and Anne—were sharing their beds with wife and husband—Camilla and Andrew.

Although Anne's adulterous affair with Andrew Parker Bowles has no direct bearing on Diana's death, it does help to illustrate the royal family's absence of moral accountability. The royal prerogative for generations of Windsors has been the

right to do anything that pleases them in pursuit
of personal satisfaction and sexual fulfillment. Anyone threatening this right automatically becomes
expendable.

Ordinary family values do not apply.

THREE

Like most women, Princess Anne never forgot the first man in her life, and when her marriage to Mark Phillips became unbearable after fifteen years, she found it easy to turn to her ex-lover Andrew Parker Bowles for emotional support and a shoulder to cry on. Their second-time-around romance coincided, totally coincidentally, with the collapse of Prince Charles's marriage to Diana following the birth of their second son, Harry. The prince had by then committed himself completely to Andrew's wife, Camilla, and the cuckolded colonel found himself at something of a loose end.

"Brother and sister and husband and wife. That's what you call a special kind of mixed foursome," said one royal observer at the time. "It was one of the best-kept royal secrets of the decade, and has taken nearly another twenty years to come out."

Following her seduction by devoted royal courtier Andrew in 1969, Princess Anne enjoyed several steamy romantic flings before and after her first marriage—mostly at her own instigation. The collapse of her marriage to Mark Phillips had begun even before the birth of their second child, Zara, in 1981. The Queen refused Anne's plea for a divorce, and rather than face a loveless and indefinite future, the princess and her husband chose to forge relationships outside their marriage.

Anne is often thought of as the staid one in the royal family, but friends say she was, and still is, a very sensual and tactile woman with a stunning figure which she usually keeps hidden under "sensible" clothes. She is almost paranoid about her privacy, and this has helped create the impression that she is something of a prude and rather straight-laced. "But the real Anne is exactly the opposite," said a friend.

Andrew Parker Bowles was Anne's first lover, and seduced the more-than-willing teenager shortly before her twentieth birthday. When her marriage went wrong in the eighties, it seemed natural to them both that Andrew provide love, affection and reassurance. He was the ideal person to help her through this sticky patch in her life.

Said a royal confidante, "It was a bizarre setup. Camilla already had Charles and Andrew, and Andrew had Camilla and was romancing Anne. It's the nearest thing to incest you can imagine. All those secret trysts in their own and friends' homes in the country. With their marriages on the rocks they just paired off again the way it was when they were all single. The only one left without a partner to play with was Diana, and the others didn't care about that. It made her feel even more isolated.

"Ignoring the unsavory aspect, which has never

been a problem with either sister or brother, Anne and Charles believed they were in a gossip-proof situation. Their secret relationships were with a married couple who were their best friends. And all three sides to this remarkable triangle were leading separate lives. Anne and Andrew had a number of favorite restaurants where they dined, and they frequently went to the cinema and theater. His appointment as commanding officer at Knightsbridge barracks gave them endless opportunities to be together.

"They would also meet at his then home, Bolehyde Manor in Wiltshire, for romantic evenings and weekends, sometimes at the same time as Camilla was keeping a rendezvous with Prince Charles at the home of a trusted friend, or at Highgrove. Diana hardly ever went there unless Charles insisted, preferring to brood alone in Kensington Palace.

"Andrew was probably the most public cuckold in the country, but very few were aware that he was enjoying a highly secret, renewed romance with the Queen's daughter. If one says his wife's lover's sister it sounds even naughtier.

"When Mark and Anne were no longer able to speak to each other, let alone be in the same house, Andrew, who is godfather to Anne's daughter, Zara, was a great morale-booster. She was at the stage where she couldn't stand Mark any longer, and at one point ordered her staff to throw all his clothes into dustbin bags and dump them in the garage when he was away on a trip.

"It was then that Andrew became invaluable. Their renewed relationship may not have had the fireworks and passion of their first encounter, but it provided the gentle romantic tenderness Anne desperately needed. Andrew escorted her to balls, parties, or simply took her for dinner alone. The two have many common interests and have a very good understanding. He may have been just a shoulder to cry on, but it was a shoulder that Anne needed then and continues to rely on.

"In many ways they were well suited and could have made a perfect couple, though Andrew had his own problems—with Camilla. I think they both accepted that, had fate dealt them an alternative hand, things might have turned out very differently for them both, and even brought them together permanently that second time around."

Said another royal insider who has known the princess for twenty-five years, "Andrew was Anne's romantic mentor when she was not yet twenty—and he was an experienced lover ten years her senior. As a Household Cavalry officer and friend of Prince Charles, he was very eligible and widely tipped to become her husband. He was her seducer and the man who awoke all that astonishing passion in her. As lovers they were well suited, for she shared his strength of passion, and had he not been a Catholic they might well have become engaged. The Queen liked him well enough to make him her silver stick in waiting."

Andrew was a supreme athlete both on the track and in the bedroom. He was a former national-hunt jockey and rode in the 1969 Grand National. "It was the talk of the mess that there wasn't a frisky horse or woman he couldn't handle. And he had a penchant for thoroughbreds. She could have had her pick of just about any man she wanted. There were a lot of young army officers at that time who would have given anything for a night with the princess.

"Her modesty, courage, and devotion to duty are well known to all, but she simply never puts her sexiness on display in public. She keeps her excellent figure hidden behind concealing clothes. And an almost obsessive demand for privacy in her off-duty life has kept this part of her personality away from the public."

Her relationships were carefully conducted in private, and rarely prompted even a mention in the tabloids. The details of her affair with her personal detective Peter Cross were well known to the royal family, including Princess Diana, and the Queen feared at the time that a serious scandal might ensue. Suave, smooth-talking and something of a womanizer, Cross was already married with two daughters when he was transferred to duties with the Royal Protection Squad. "Peter was a bit green and gauche when he first joined the princess's staff," said a former servant, "but what he lacked in dress sense and social graces he made up for with his essential, down-to-earth masculinity which the princess simply adored."

"Even though he was a royal detective," revealed a former colleague, "he was not the most discreet of men. If he and Anne had been allowed to continue with their relationship, the palace was terrified he would brag about it and plunge the royal family into a major scandal."

Cross was called to Scotland Yard for a meeting with Wilfred Gibson, the assistant commissioner in charge of royal protection, and sacked. He was accused of being overfamiliar with the princess, and

was told he had "misunderstood her friendship."
Mark Phillips claimed that it was he who had Cross
transferred to other duties after he discovered
Cross's true feelings for the princess, but the decision was actually made by Establishment figures
who chose not to contradict Mark's claims.

Even after Cross quit the force and joined an insurance company, his relationship with Anne continued. "It started with kisses and hand-holding,"
revealed Cross later. But the affair quickly developed and they met once a month, either in an
empty cottage on the Gatcombe Estate or at the
home of Cross's friend who loaned the lovers his
keys. Mark complained about the embarrassing
publicity, but all that earned him was the brunt of
Anne's legendary temper. Mark was told to mind
his own business.

Eventually the affair dwindled into nothing and
Cross began a new relationship; but for a few years
he seemed to be the most important man in
Princess Anne's life.

"An army officer at Buckingham Palace amused
the princess for a while," explained a former aide,
"then came her resurrected romance with Brigadier
Parker Bowles."

For a time it suited them both, but Anne was
looking for someone new with whom to share her
life. In 1986, Commander Timothy Lawrence was
detailed to join Buckingham Palace as an equerry
to the Queen. Aged just thirty and not very experienced with girls, he had a boyish air of innocence.
Anne first saw him there on a visit to her mother:
suddenly she was confronted by a new and eligible
figure in military uniform, and romance gave way
to a more urgent passion. Soon a new joke was

making the rounds below stairs that the duties an equerry to the Queen had to fulfill were equivalent to a thirty-mile run—but without the boots, uniform or rucksack.

There is a consensus among Timothy and Anne's friends that the well-mannered, career officer—known to his naval chums as Tiger Tim—was seduced by the princess. The tiger, they agreed, was no match for the royal tigress.

Tim's feelings were so intense that he felt the need to commit them to paper. Four intimate letters proclaiming his passionate feelings for his royal mistress were stolen that April—and precipitated an official separation from Mark Phillips. Anne had valued the letters so much—reading and re-reading them over and over again—that she couldn't bear to have them out of her sight. She carried them everywhere in her briefcase, and it was from there that they were stolen and passed to a tabloid newspaper.

This time, when she went to her mother pleading for an official separation, she found the Queen not only compliant but encouraging. She turned down Tim's offer to resign as equerry and, as an apparent signal of her approval of her daughter's lover, insisted he join their Ascot party and cruise with them on the royal yacht to Scotland.

In March 1991, the threat of a paternity suit by horsewoman Heather Tonkin ensured that Anne and Mark's divorce—undefended after a two-year separation—should go through in August that year. The divorce itself was simple. But Anne's demands on her husband were tough. Mark received a lump sum. In return he had to give up any claim to Anne's, or the Queen's, property. The princess had custody of the children and Mark had to sign a confidentiality agreement. The divorce severed virtually every connection between Mark and the royal family.

To most royals, it was as though he had never existed—the same royals, no doubt, who would wish in a few years time that the same could happen with Princess Diana.

FOUR

"Oh, it's a boy. And it's even got red hair!"

Charles's brief visit to Diana's hospital bedside, and his even briefer verbal reaction—reported in its entirety above—to the birth of their second son before dashing off to play polo indicated to many, including the princess herself, the real moment when the Waleses' marriage was irretrievably lost.

With his perfect mistress in place, Charles would have remained in his loveless marriage for the rest of his life and counted himself extremely lucky by royal standards. What had no part in his idyllic marital scenario was permitting Diana a liaison of her own. What was good for the gander was, in the prince's opinion, unacceptable for the goose. As a future king, he felt entitled not only to have a mistress, but also to be as open about it as he pleased. On the other hand, his double standards demanded that his wife be utterly faithful. Ironically, he judged

her by his own standards and found her guilty of
infidelity with a man called Philip Dunne.

Dunne was the merchant-banker son of the lord
lieutenant of Herefordshire. He had been introduced to Diana and Charles by newlyweds Prince
Andrew and Sarah Ferguson when they had joined
them at Klosters for their annual skiing holiday.
They had turned up with a couple of spare men,
one of whom was Dunne. Diana had found him
charming and amusing and had spent a night
chatting to him at a local discotheque. Another
evening was spent playing schoolgirl games which
involved mild flirtation, but nothing more serious.

Back in England, Dunne invited some of the skiing party for a weekend house party at his parents'
home, and when the press discovered that Charles
was not present, and neither were Dunne's parents, they concluded, wrongly, that Diana had finally found someone to help her through a rocky
period in her marriage.

Charles was initially suspicious, but when Dunne
explained that a whole group of guests had spent
the weekend with him, he concluded, rightly, that
Diana had not begun an affair with the younger
man, though she clearly found him attractive. And
had it not been for Charles's own typically selfish
behavior at the wedding of the Marquis of Worcester,
son of the Duke of Beaufort, in June 1987, that is
how it would have remained.

He spent the whole evening following the actual
marriage ceremony talking to Camilla and ignored
Diana completely. To be so publicly humiliated by
the prince, yet again, was more than Diana could
stomach and, white-lipped with anger, she pulled a
surprised, but not reluctant, Philip Dunne on to

the dance floor where they danced wildly together until dawn—long after Charles had slipped away with Camilla. Angered by his wife's petulant and deliberate exhibitionism, which he believed was her attempt to embarrass him by flaunting her infidelity with Dunne in front of his friends and a generous portion of high-society England, Charles was now convinced that the couple had slept together.

Pausing only to collect Camilla, Charles headed for Balmoral on September 22 and began a separation from Diana which would end in questions being asked in parliament. Thirty-seven days went by, during which time the prince avoided all contact with his wife and sons. A brief get-together for a visit to Dyfed in Wales, which had been the victim of appalling floods, failed to convince the press that their marriage was in anything but dire straits. After six hours, during which they barely spoke a word to each other, Diana returned to London and Charles went back to Balmoral—and Camilla.

By February 1989, Diana was feeling sufficiently strong to have her first, and only, confrontation with Camilla. Treatment from Guy's Hospital eating-disorders specialist Doctor Maurice Lipsedge had enabled her to bring the bulimia under control and, feeling more confident than she had done in years, Diana decided it was time to take Camilla Parker Bowles head on. She chose a party at Sir James Goldsmith's home in Ormley Lodge, Richmond Park, to celebrate the fortieth birthday of Camilla's sister, Annabel Elliott, as her battleground.

Charles, according to Diana's personal protection officer Ken Wharfe, had not expected her to attend, and until the last moment—in the car taking them to the event—tried to dissuade her. But she coolly insisted, and caused surprise and even consternation among the other guests when she walked in with the prince. After dinner, Diana realized that Charles and Camilla had gone off together; summoning Ken Wharfe, she went downstairs in search of them, though a number of the guests tried to persuade her not to.

They found Charles and Camilla sitting in a softly lit children's den, deep in conversation. At this point Ken Wharfe—not wanting to be part of a marital row—excused himself and waited by the basement steps outside the room. Minutes later, Diana appeared. She told him that she had confronted Camilla about her relationship with Charles. "It wasn't a fight," she said. "Calm, deathly calm, I said to Camilla, 'I'm sorry I'm in the way. I obviously am in the way and it must be hell for both of you, but I do know what is going on. Don't treat me like an idiot.' " Diana then returned to the party with her head held high, ignoring the fact that her confrontation with Camilla was the talk of the room. Charles and his mistress returned shortly afterward, looking shaken, and spent the rest of the evening circulating separately.

On the journey home, Diana could only repeat over and over to a silent Prince Charles, "How could you have done this to me? It was so humiliating. How could you?" Wharfe believed that what tore the princess in two, wrecking her emotionally, was their readiness to humble her publicly without apparent remorse. From that night on she only ever referred to Camilla by her new nickname: the Rottweiler.

The tension within the household became so unbearable that Wendy Berry's son, James, quit as a valet. He told her, "I've got to the stage where I just can't respect the prince or the princess any more. Their unhappy lives are destroying my own, and I don't want to be caught in the crossfire."

At that time, Charles had more than forty silver-framed photographs adorning various surfaces in his private study at Highgrove. There were photographs of the royal family and his sons, and various pictures of his favorite horses and dogs. But there was not a single picture of his wife—ironically the world's most photographed woman.

In a sad little memoir Andrew Jacques, the local police constable who had guarded Highgrove for four years, wrote that the only times Charles and Diana met was at meal times, which very often ended in a blazing row for all to hear. "They never smile, laugh, or do anything together. In four years I only ever saw him kiss her goodbye once, and that was a peck on the cheek."

The following summer, Charles suffered a ghastly tumble from his polo pony. He broke his arm so badly that part of the bone was protruding from the flesh below his elbow. It was a complicated break in two places, and set so badly the first time that the bone had to be rebroken and set with the aid of a metal pin and bone from the prince's hip, which was grafted on. Add to this a tendon which became trapped in the fracture, with the bone healing around it, and for Charles it signified a long period of permanent pain.

Diana was with him for both operations in July and September, and personally escorted him back to Highgrove. But each time, after about an hour, she left him there and returned to London, with hardly a civil word having been exchanged between them. Moments after she left, Mrs. Parker Bowles would be driven in through the gates of Highgrove by Charles's detective.

For most of that summer Charles and Camilla lived at Highgrove virtually as man and wife. Friends viewed her as his official hostess in Gloucestershire, and she organized parties and dinners in his home. When Diana made one of her very infrequent and unwelcome visits there, Camilla would dash home until her rival had gone back to London, and then resume her place as Charles's nurse and comforter.

Despite this blissful domestic scene, Charles was increasingly subject to bouts of deep depression, a condition, his doctors believed, which could have been brought on by delayed shock from his polo accident. However, for whatever reason, it was now Charles's turn to suffer from the pressure. By the end of that summer he was displaying all the symptoms of going through a nervous breakdown, and he was unable to fulfill an official function of any kind for four months.

He holed up in Balmoral with Camilla and Patsy Palmer-Tompkinson, and scared friends and courtiers alike by sinking ever deeper into depression. But even at such a low ebb he was still unable to find any blame, within his own behavior, to explain his marital problems. It was all Diana's fault, he maintained, and his friends commiserated. It was Diana, they agreed, who received all the adulation and press attention, and Diana who devoted every second, it appeared, to upstaging her dejected husband. She had become his nemesis, his torturer, his personal hell on earth. However hard he tried to capture the public imagination, nobody appeared to care a damn. All they ever wanted was Diana. The damage to his pride was substantial, and his jealousy of his despised wife became over-whelming.

After two months in Scotland, followed by a few brief hours with Diana and their sons, Charles flew to the South of France. The ache in his arm still troubled him, and he now suffered an added pain in his hip from where the bone had been removed to graft his broken arm. He took with him a phys-iotherapist who helped reduce the aches and pains, but he could find no one to relieve his men-tal anguish.

After a week the prince returned home, too restless and troubled to enjoy the sun and the stunning views from Baroness Louise de Waldner's chateau near Avignon which she had made avail-able to him at Camilla's urging. What tormented Charles the most was that he genuinely believed Diana had understood the ground rules of royal marriage before their wedding. It was for this rea-son that he was so bewildered, and angered, by the constant tantrums surrounding his relationship with Mrs. Parker Bowles.

Diana, on the other hand, amazingly still be-lieved that the marriage could be saved, and told her confidants, including her royal protection offi-cer, that if she showed enough love for her hus-band then he would surely start to love her back and no longer feel the need for a mistress. For her it was still not too late to rule out a "happily ever after" scenario. Or at least so she maintained.

Diana's displays of affection were rare, but occa-sionally, said Wendy Berry, she would run up to him out in the garden and fling her arms around him. Charles would either appear embarrassed, or make a half-hearted attempt to reciprocate—but he always seemed distracted when he did so. When he did this, Diana would storm off, leaving Charles calling after her, "Darling, come back. Of course I want to hug you."

She even proposed trying for another baby, and outwardly claimed she saw no problem in achieving this, even though she and the prince had not shared a marital bed for more than three years. Charles's response to her baby proposal was to disappear to Florence on another holiday with Camilla. It was his way of drawing up the battle lines for the start of one of the stormiest periods of their marriage.

Princess Diana's reaction was to embark on her first real love affair.

She had met James Hewitt, a dashing young cavalry officer in the Life Guards, a charming and very likeable man, in the summer of 1986. Diana was terrified of horses and had mistrusted them from childhood. Hewitt gave her riding lessons until she became fairly competent and no longer afraid of the beasts.

He was handsome. More importantly, he was energetic and passionate—all the attributes missing in Charles. She adored him. He also taught her about love, and after two years they had developed an intense sexual relationship. For the first time in her life, Diana experienced in full what it was like to be with someone she loved and trusted and who loved her in equal measure.

Several people close to Diana, including her personal detective Ken Wharfe, say that Charles knew exactly what was going on between Hewitt and his wife. But he was happy for it to continue because it suited him: if another man was keeping his wife satisfied, it was less trouble for him.

They would frequently meet at his mother's Devon cottage or in Kensington Palace where Hewitt would often spend the night. The princess was blissfully happy, and insisted on giving Hewitt many thousands of pounds in cash and gifts, including a new car. She bought him clothes, spending fortunes on Savile Row suits and handmade shoes. She chose shirts for him, and expensive cufflinks.

Hewitt was not exactly displaying conduct becoming an officer of the Life Guards, but it made Diana happy—and all her staff and friends remarked on her new determination, confidence and gaiety. Charles too noted the changes in his wife and recognized how the new "arrangement" in their marriage was helping them both to enjoy a happier, and certainly more relaxed, domestic life.

However, despite these positive changes, when she was not with Hewitt the princess still looked, at times, heart-rendingly sad and lonely. "There's nothing I can do to reach Charles," she told one confidant. "It just tears me apart to love him and know he loves someone else and doesn't give a damn about me." The hypocrisy of her situation in pursuing an affair with Hewitt while complaining of Charles's adultery with Camilla never occurred to Diana. The prince's betrayal of her simply exceeded any other hurt she had suffered in her short life, and returning such hurt to him in kind was never seen as sin, but justice.

On the negative side, for years now, ever since

her affair became public knowledge, cruel and totally unsubstantiated rumors have circulated at
candlelit dinner parties in Chelsea and over afternoon tea in the drawing rooms of Belgravia. This
upper-class gossip focused on the similarity between Major Hewitt and young Prince Harry.
There is no doubt that there is a strong likeness,
but Prince Harry also happens to share the same
look and mischievous expression as Diana's younger
sister. Also, we are assured, James Hewitt and Princess Diana did not meet and fall in love until after
Harry was born, although unfounded rumors still
persist that their real first meeting took place long
before that.

Stranger still, then, is the fact that in Hewitt's
bedroom, at his country home in Wiltshire, only
one picture is on display. It is a framed photograph of Prince Harry. Clearly Major Hewitt has a
good reason for favoring this photograph above
all others to gaze at last thing at night and first in
the morning. Perhaps it is simply that he retains a
strong and lasting admiration for the spirited
young prince. When I asked him he declined, very
politely, to give an explanation.

Diana's weekdays had become dictated by
William's school hours, for she saw it as her duty to
drive him to school and pick him up each day.
Newspaper editors universally approved of this, because her constant changes of outfit provided
front-page pictures on an almost daily basis.

Charles was, for the most part, content with the
one mistress, although he did sometimes have

friends line up a female companion—an old con-
quest or a royal groupie—for his amusement.
Diana, on the other hand, starved of love and
male attention for so many years, was unable to re-
sist playing the field, and for the rest of her life
would encourage several suitors at any one time.

Their lifestyles evolved a regular pattern at that
time. At weekends, if she and the boys made one
of their infrequent trips to Highgrove, it was usually the signal for Charles to go hunting or to polo,
his standard excuse for visiting Camilla. He
seemed loath to be under the same roof as Diana,
said the staff at Highgrove. Her revenge, always
producing spectacular results, was to continue to
upstage him on every possible occasion. When he
made a speech on education she made one on
AIDS. When he tried to seize a photo opportunity
playing cello during a visit to an Australian music
college, Diana stole the show by hammering out
the opening bars to a famous Russian piano con-
certo on an old upright. She outshone her husband, and indeed the whole royal family, on every
occasion and whenever it took her fancy to do so.

Even when it came to using their children to
score points off each other, the princess had no
scruples. Charles was en route to Italy for a holiday
with Camilla when he was told that the three-year-
old Prince Harry had been rushed to hospital for a
hernia operation. He was personally reassured by
Diana that it wasn't necessary for him to fly home.
There was no danger to their son. It was not until
the next day that Charles discovered how easily he
had been duped by his wife. Diana had spent the
night at the hospital, sleeping in a chair "to be

close to my little boy." Newspapers labelled her "a saint," while Charles was left fuming, once more classified as the villain of the piece.

But it seemed he had learned little from these experiences when Prince William was hit on the head with a golf club by another boy. He and Diana had rushed their separate ways to be by their son's side, and later accompanied him to Great Ormond Street Children's Hospital in London, where specialists had advised he undergo urgent surgery. Having been told there was nothing he could do until after the operation was completed and William recovered from the general anesthetic, the prince left, after strong urging from Diana, to fulfill a longstanding engagement at the Royal Opera House. Predictably for everyone except Charles, the headlines the next day demanded WHAT KIND OF DAD ARE YOU? Charles's answer, by now just as predictable, was to withdraw even further from his family and concentrate more on his affair with Camilla.

It still riled Diana when the prince paraded his paramour in front of friends, though she now rarely made a fuss. However, she felt some places should remain Camilla-free zones, and one such place was the memorial service for Leonora Knatchbull, the six-year-old daughter of Lord and Lady Romsey, who had died of cancer. When she learned he had invited Camilla to attend this very private event, she was furious. Diana had cuddled Leonora when the brave little girl had watched the Trooping of the Colour from the balcony of Buckingham Palace shortly before her death. As she left St. James's Palace, Diana was photographed in tears—tears of rage. In great distress, she made the point vigorously to Charles in their short drive to Kensington

Palace, where she locked herself in the bathroom, still in tears. He was unmoved by her misery and went out, leaving the young princes to slide paper hankies under the bathroom door to their mother.

Early in 1991, Diana was forced to take the boys skiing alone because at the last moment Charles had pleaded an urgent need to prepare several speeches for forthcoming engagements. He chose to ignore heavy criticism both from palace advisers —who still hoped to project an image of family togetherness—and the press. He claimed duty had to take precedence, but in reality he was meeting with Camilla in Scotland, having been secretly supported by the Queen Mother who offered them the use of Birkhall, her house on the Balmoral Estate.

In private, all the royal women tended to sympathize with Prince Charles over Diana's refusal to be compliant about Camilla. Royal men were traditionally entitled to enjoy their mistresses without the meddlesome and irksome interference or emotional opposition of their wives. Throughout this period Charles and his father, Prince Philip, found themselves in rare agreement, and were resolute in their shared belief that their bitterness over Diana's recalcitrance was utterly justified. It was the princess, they maintained, who was being unreasonable in her refusal to accept the normality of Charles's affair with Camilla.

Diana's visit to Lech in January, when the boys had their first skiing lessons, had not gone by without one interesting relationship developing—that between Diana and her cousin by marriage. Viscount Linley—Princess Margaret's son—was then single and, at twenty-nine, just four months younger than the Princess of Wales. He was there ostensibly as a chaperone, and stayed with Diana and the two princes. She was starved of affection and desperately missing James Hewitt, who was fighting with his regiment in the Gulf War.

Charles, a fanatical skier himself, was annoyed when he learned that Harry had already mastered the art of downhill skiing and that he had missed this experience in his adventurous young son's development. He was also said to have been white-lipped with fury when told of the scurrilous rumors emanating from Lech which featured suggestions of provocative nighttime activities involving Viscount Linley and his wife. I am told that his cousin's denials that anything untoward had taken place were not in themselves sufficient to calm his temper. Nor did they prevent the rumors from circulating. Charles was convinced Diana and his cousin had become lovers and denounced them, loudly, to his closest companions.

The mere thought of such scandalous tales bursting into the public domain spread panic around the corridors of the twin palaces. At the trial of butler Paul Burrell, the court was about to hear revelations about Diana's close bond with David Linley when the case collapsed. Linley did become extremely close to the princess during the time they stayed together in Lech—and throughout 1991—and wrote many intimate letters to his "Darling Diana." Only one letter survived. The others are believed to have been shredded by Diana's mother, Frances Shand-Kydd, on the day after her daughter's death in 1997.

The one intact letter was seized at Burrell's home in Cheshire during a police raid in January

2001. It had been with her other "Crown Jewels." The jury was invited to read the letter themselves in an attempt to prevent the contents, which were said to be extremely frank, being disclosed to the public. It was known, however, that the letter ended with the endearment, "masses of love from David."

Had the case not collapsed it is almost certain that the letter's contents, and possibly those of other letters which were understood to be equally frank, would have been revealed in open court when Burrell entered the witness box. The royal family was, understandably, extremely unhappy at the prospect of a close link being disclosed between Diana and another royal. It was an added reason to keep Diana's "insurance" from falling into the public domain.

After the Burrell trial fiasco Viscount Linley, now a married father of two, said he and the princess were "nothing more than good friends." "I didn't have an intimate relationship with her," he said. But at that stage, with the Queen having saved his reputation from being shredded in court, it is hardly likely he would have confessed to an adulterous relationship with his cousin-in-law!

At the time the letters were written, Viscount Linley was still living with his mother, Princess Margaret, in Kensington Palace. She and Diana had neighboring apartments in the same building.

The royal visit to India and the death of Diana's father, Lord Spencer, were the two events which were ultimately to bring about the beginning of the end of the Waleses' marriage.

Inexplicably, Charles and his aides turned down

the opportunity to have his photograph taken with Diana in front of the Taj Mahal. He had once promised the Indian people that some day he would bring the Princess of Wales to see the incredible tomb built by the seventeenth-century emperor Shah Jahan for his late wife. Photographs taken with this ethereal vision in white marble as a backdrop might, alone, have convinced the world that the royal marriage still had a chance. But Charles's defunct romantic antennae failed to divine this golden opportunity, and he chose instead to address a group of very unromantic business leaders in Delhi while Diana posed alone—abandoned, said the press—in front of this symbol of true love.

In truth, Diana had reveled in this fabulous solo photographic coup, but to the world's media she felt it necessary to devise a "revenge" on the man they had described as her "neglectful and uncaring" spouse. The revenge she devised was painfully cruel to watch and was, without doubt, the most devastating public put-down of any man by his wife.

It came on the eve of St. Valentine's Day and at the end of a polo match in Jaipur, and was executed, as royal reporter James Whittaker recorded, in front of 100 professional cameramen and 5,000 laughing Indians. Charles's team had won, and he dutifully lined up with its members to receive the winner's trophy from the princess.

Wrote Whitaker, "With triumph in her eyes, Diana waited until her husband's lips were almost on hers; then she turned her head away. Not suddenly so as to allow Charles to pull back—no, it was much more calculating than that. Instead she moved her head to the left, slowly.

"Charles, who knew the world would see what happened next—television was there too—politely and gallantly tried to follow Diana's turning head. He chased it all the way around until he could reach no further without falling over. He ended up kissing Diana half in midair, half on her gold earring."

He was still fuming when he returned to England and told a sympathetic Camilla, "That's the last time she holds me up to ridicule." Both agreed it was time he went on the public relations offensive.

In April, after spending a week with Camilla in Milan, Charles flew to join Diana and the princes in Lech in Austria on their skiing holiday. Diana was ordered to stay out of the way and William and Harry were waiting outside the Arlberg Hotel for Charles's arrival. The press was treated to two days of father-and-sons pictures, which made the world's front pages, and Charles was able to congratulate himself on making the PR releases ahead of his wife.

Then came the news that Earl Spencer had died in hospital.

After a massive row, and finally only after the direct intervention of the Queen who personally issued an order to her daughter-in-law, did Diana agree to Charles flying home on the same plane as herself. But this was only, it seemed to everyone in retrospect, so that she would have an available fall-guy foil for the arrival pictures she had so carefully choreographed. At Northolt Airport she snatched away all his hard-won PR points of the previous two days and made him look an insensitive oaf. She simply waited until he had descended the airplane steps and was deep in conversation with an aide, before making her dramatic appearance.

Diana emerged from the doorway of the plane, carrying a heavy bag in one hand, took a couple of faltering paces, and paused at the top of the steps, looking grief-stricken, waiting for the flashbulbs to flare. It was, for the entire world to see, as though in her moment of personal tragedy the sad princess had no one to offer a helping hand—least of all her husband.

For the funeral—which Diana had, quite unrealistically, asked him not to attend—Charles insisted on sending his own wreath. The princess, who had not been to Althorp since 1989 for her brother's wedding, and who had avoided meeting with her father on several occasions when he called at Kensington Palace, sent her own wreath too. On the card she wrote of "missing her darling daddy." "She hardly ever saw him," said Sue Ingram, Raine Spencer's tight-faced assistant pointedly.

Unwanted by the Spencers, Charles flew to the funeral at Althorp alone in a Wessex helicopter of the Queen's Flight. Diana traveled in a car driven by her personal detective Ken Wharfe, who recalled her telling him at the time, "He's going to turn my father's funeral into a charade, Ken. It's so false."

Afterward, Prince Charles managed to upset his namesake—Charles, the new Earl Spencer—by telling him how lucky he was to have inherited so young. The earl, who had just buried his father, said that in making this observation the prince did not seem to appreciate how he felt about his loss. "I wish I had inherited so young," Charles told him with a characteristic lack of sensitivity. While he obviously did not wish his mother, the Queen, any harm, least of all her death, it is a glaring example of his tactlessness.

The prince left early by helicopter to return to Camilla in Gloucestershire, and sent Raine Spencer a handwritten five-page letter of condolence, while Diana, having agreed with her brother that Raine should perhaps consider alternative residential arrangements, returned to Kensington Palace with Ken Wharfe.

The following month, Diana flew to Cairo for a series of solo public engagements in Egypt. Her Queen's Flight aircraft—to her deep annoyance—made a detour to Ankara to drop off Charles who had arranged a further holiday in Turkey with Camilla. She was still seething with rage when she told her host, the British Ambassador, and his guests that she expected to be just Lady Di again by the time her husband was eventually crowned. This was seven months before the end of her marriage was officially announced, and proved a total conversation-stopper.

Yet despite her emotionally charged state, Diana turned Egypt into another spectacular media triumph with a series of stunning photographs using the pyramids, the Sphinx and the great palace at Luxor as backdrops. The only downside for the princess was that, this time, the press had failed to spot Camilla alongside Charles during their Turkish holiday. It was hardly a very satisfying revenge, but on her way home she refused to collect him in Ankara, even though the pilot told her they would fly almost directly over the Turkish capital. Charles had to order that her aircraft do a fast turnaround when it reached England, and return to pick him up.

The princess's comments—usually fueled by anger or provoked by her husband's boorishness, especially those like her bombshell in Cairo—continued to make headlines and constantly seemed to catch Charles and his aides by surprise. It is certain that none of their friends or the palace staff had the slightest inkling that she had secretly planned to unleash a bombshell of such mega proportions that it would deal a devastating blow to the monarchy and be the means by which she would break free of her disastrous marriage.

Andrew Morton's biography *Diana: Her True Story* had an even greater impact on the royals than the princess had dreamed possible. Her in-laws were not just rocked to the foundations, but were in danger of falling down entirely. The royal family en masse pointed the finger of blame at Diana but she, slightly fearful now of what she had put in motion eighteen months earlier, vehemently denied cooperating with the author, or encouraging her friends to help in any way. She stuck to this story throughout, even though it was untrue and she had supplied Andrew Morton with many hours of tape recordings in which she clearly spelled out her problems and placed the blame for her failed marriage squarely at Camilla's door.

It was a thrust of such wounding proportions that it might well have proved fatal to the House of Windsor—and it was delivered deliberately, albeit under intense provocation, by a woman who was an absolute royalist, and whose children's future depended to a great extent on the monarchy's survival. To Prince Philip it was a devastating blow. He saw all his hard work in reshaping and consolidating the family since 1947 being wiped out by Diana's ill-judged revelations. It stirred feelings of real hatred for the first time, I was told.

While understandable as an act of revenge against Charles and Camilla, it was at the same time a vain, childish and extremely stupid act, and was one which Diana was to regret deeply, for it did all the royals and their loyal courtiers and staff lasting and fundamental damage. But there could be no denying that, on a different level, her plan was superbly successful. The ability of the palace or the Establishment to control her, or her marriage, had been removed.

But what of the cost? Diana had helped to expose the corrupt side of royalty and to take away the family's credibility. Walter Bagehot once cautioned royal writers, "We must not let in daylight upon magic." Diana had not just pulled back the curtains and let the harsh light of reality flood in, she had ripped them away and exposed how the trick was done.

Of one thing there was no doubt. After the Morton book the problems between Diana and Charles became insoluble. In the winter of 1990–91, Charles and Diana had grown so full of hatred for each other that the Highgrove staff feared for the safety of both. They both found each other's company so offensive that barely a civil word passed between them, explained Wendy Berry. On one occasion, Diana was sitting on the stairs sobbing when Charles shouted, "For God's sake, Diana, come here and talk to me."

"I hate you, Charles," she shrieked. "I fucking hate you."

It was a typical exchange.

Diana herself, at this time, remained immensely popular, though public opinion of Charles had swung to an all-time low. He had zero support. Wearily the Queen summoned the couple to a private meeting, at which a formal separation was suggested by both. Her answer was that they go, with the princes, on one final family holiday and at least try to patch up their differences. Neither believed such a holiday would achieve anything—except perhaps add a few more scars to their marriage. But neither was prepared to refuse the Queen's request, and so a further Greek cruise on John Latsis's luxury yacht was agreed. Its main attraction was that it was so large Charles and Diana did not actually have to meet while aboard.

After initially spending hours hiding in a lifeboat and sobbing, and then threatening to fly home at the first port of call—tantrums that Diana's long-suffering private detective Ken Wharfe was left to sort out—the princess enjoyed long days of water sports with her children, while Charles spent many hours of each day talking to Camilla on the telephone in his cabin.

Camilla, discovering at firsthand the pressures from the fourth estate that Diana had endured for ten years, was in temporary exile abroad, having dodged the British press's formidable attempts to interview her, and announced she would only return after the fuss died down. A consolation came at Christmas when Charles bought his mistress a beautiful diamond necklace as a present. It was a further slap in the face for Diana who, knowing what he had bought Camilla, found his gift to her was a cheap set of paste gems!

The Establishment prayed for a miracle to take the heat off Mrs. Parker Bowles and the prince, and tumble Diana from her elevated public pedestal. The scandal which would provide that miracle was, in fact, already in place—put together by officers of the Secret Intelligence Service—and would prove almost as sensational as *Diana: Her True Story*. Their allegedly unwitting pawn was an unlikely candidate for scandal-mongering. Cyril Reeman, a retired bank manager, whose bizarre late-night hobby was listening to other people's telephone conversations, recorded an incredible chat between Princess Diana and her car-dealer friend James Gilby.

It was originally obtained by the Secret Intelligence Service from a phone tap on Diana's telephone inside Kensington Palace. Bugging at such a high level would usually require the sanction of the prime minister, who at this time was John Major. The SIS claimed their concern was protection of the princess.

Publication of the tape in the *Sun* could not have come at a better time for Charles and Camilla. It was, in short, a godsend.

The *Sun*'s quirky editor had chosen to dub it the Squidgy Tape.

FIVE

Publication of the Squidgy Tape in 1992 resulted in Diana, Princess of Wales, being blamed for the problems in her marriage for the first time.

The royals had been aware from the mid-eighties that for security reasons it had become necessary for the security services to monitor and record all telephone conversations as a routine precaution, although it was understood that nothing of a personal nature would be kept on record. Initiating this policy meant recording all telephone and some face-to-face conversations both inside and outside the royal residences.

It was certainly not explained that copies of some royal conversations, if deemed relevant, would be forwarded, on a regular basis, to the security services of the United States. Nor was it explained, or even leaked until many years later, that the Americans were also eavesdropping on royal conversations through the NSA using its ultra-secret, Star Wars-style system known as the ECHELON project.

The National Security Agency, which was secretly created in 1952 by President Truman, admitted to the *Washington Post* that they possessed files on Princess Diana partly composed of interrupted telephone conversations. It is known that the NSA's mandate was expanded by President Reagan to include information systems and operations security, and to achieve its goals, an automated global interruption-relay system, code-named ECHELON, was developed by the NSA and is now operated by the intelligence organizations in five nations: the United States, the United Kingdom, Canada, Australia and New Zealand.

The existence of the ECHELON project is still not acknowledged by the United States government, although European Union and Australian government committees have officially admitted its existence. ECHELON monitors upward of three billion communications each day, including telephone calls, e-mails, Internet downloads and satellite transmissions. There are separate search lists for each country. They siphon out what is valuable using artificial intelligence programs.

Because James Gilby, then a salesman for Lotus cars, used his pet name for Diana—"Squidgy"—during their twenty-three-minute conversation, this was the name label used to identify the tape. The phone call—to Gilby in his car—was purported to have been picked up by an amateur radio buff, Cyril Reeman, randomly roving through the airwaves. The chances of this happening are extremely small;

an amateur managing to tape all twenty-three minutes of the conversation with no gaps, when mo-
bile-phone networks continually shift frequency
during operation, is technically impossible.

That the phone call itself took place on New
Year's Eve 1989, and the amateur radio enthusiast
recorded it on January 4, 1990, is clearly also impossible. Telephone signals do not hang about in
the ether for ninety-six hours. Cellnet, which operated the network then used by Gilby, categorically
denied that the call could have been recorded in
the manner claimed.

The only explanation is that the call was recorded
from a bug or other listening device in Kensington
Palace, and then broadcast on a fixed wavelength
four days later so it could easily be picked up by an
amateur radio buff. In the intervening days, the
tape had been electronically cleaned. The sound
of other traffic and reflected noise on the road
where Gilby took the call had been removed to
make the voices of him and Diana more easily understood. The tape was examined by a leading
technical expert in national security matters. In
his opinion the tape had been "cleaned" using a
special machine with which he was familiar. The
machine used was not particularly expensive: it
cost about £30,000. But it has an interesting rarity
factor. He revealed there are only two such machines
in Britain: one belongs to MI5 and the other to
MI6.

Further, also in his opinion, no non-government
department or organization would be allowed to
buy the machine from its manufacturer.

The two branches of the British secret service—

MI5 which concentrates on problems in Britain, and MI6 which deals with overseas situations—are also the only ones with the equipment to have bugged Kensington Palace and rebroadcast the tape at a later date.

Princess Diana's personal protection officer at that time, Ken Wharfe, revealed a decade later that the intelligence services routinely taped her telephone conversations. He revealed that at least two sets of Diana tapes are in existence, "recordings of the same conversation made on different days by different radio buffs." Wharfe believes that they were transmitted on a number of occasions in order to make sure they were picked up.

In the rather tawdry conversation, fully featured in the *Sun* in August 1992, Diana mentions her fear of becoming pregnant with Gilby's child, demonstrating the sexual nature of their relationship. It was not a statement the royal family could dismiss as being an exaggeration or a misinterpretation, as they had with Andrew Morton's book. This was straight from the horse's mouth—and no one who heard it had any doubt that from this point on an official separation of the prince and princess must follow, sooner rather than later.

Diana had also unequivocally revealed her feelings about the royal family in repeating to Gilby one of her frequently mouthed comments: "Bloody hell. After all I've done for that fucking family." It was a phrase heard dozens of times over the years by staff, friends and her personal detectives.

Prince Charles had the good sense to keep quiet, and almost certainly thanked God that the Squidgy Tape had taken the pressure off him and

Camilla. Diana meanwhile, though highly embarrassed by the publication of her very private conversation with a lover, had long since dropped Gilby and transferred her attention to another man, art dealer Oliver Hoare. Her affair with James Hewitt had also foundered after a brief renaissance during the Gulf War when she sent him luxury food hampers, pornographic magazines and steamy, handwritten love letters. For a time it had satisfied Diana's romantic need to have a sweetheart bravely facing the dangers of war. But when Major Hewitt returned to London, Diana found the old buzz was no longer there, and she suggested they "cool it" for a while. After that she did not reply to his phone messages.

Oliver Hoare was married to Diane, an extremely wealthy woman in her own right, and the couple had met Charles and Diana at a function at Windsor Castle. The prince had struck up an immediate friendship with Hoare and the four of them dined together occasionally at one or other of their homes. Oliver Hoare also knew the Parker Bowleses, and initially Diana was attracted to him because she believed he might explain the mysterious attraction Camilla exercised over her husband—something which the princess never did understand.

Hoare was clearly flattered by her attentions, and willingly agreed to a series of assignations, though he neither expected nor wanted it to lead to anything serious. Diana, on the other hand, became temporarily besotted with the thirty-nine-year-old—as she did with all the men to whom she was attracted. This led to her taking risks, for Diana needed the constant reassurance that she was the most memorable woman in her lover's life. On one occasion, to give Hoare a taste of the "unforgettable" aspect of an affair with the Princess of Wales, she arrived on his doorstep wearing a full-length fur coat, which she flung open, revealing that underneath she was stark naked—except, that is, for a diamond necklace.

Despite stunts like this, and though they spent nights together at Kensington Palace, or in the homes of mutual and discreet friends, she agonized, correctly, that he did not reciprocate her love. These doubts made her irritable and unapproachable, even to her favorites. She was definitely in no mood to give more than short shrift to the palace aide who brought outline plans for a proposed "romantic" visit to the East with her husband. She told the man not to be stupid and to go away.

Incredibly, despite the parlous state of the Waleses' marriage, certain palace aides really believed they could still organize a fence-mending operation on their nonexistent relationship, and had proposed a "kiss and make up" tour of South Korea. Diana was not even speaking to Charles at this stage, and announced that in the name of all honesty she saw no reason to go. The Foreign Office, her senior staff and finally Ken Wharfe were recruited to try and persuade her to change her mind, but with no success. In the end it took a tough talking-to by the Queen to get Diana to capitulate, though then only very reluctantly.

With hindsight it was agreed that it would have been far more sensible to have canceled the visit, or to have sent Prince Charles alone. The whole, pointless exercise was a disaster for the royals and a deep embarrassment to the couple's hosts—the people of South Korea. With no consideration for anyone's feelings but their own, the Waleses indulged themselves in a massive shouting match on board the royal flight as it descended into Seoul airport, and when they finally emerged flushed, angry and scowling, it set the tone for the next five days: sullen, uncooperative and bleak.

It was, even the media agreed, a sad and sorry ending to the fairy-tale marriage which it had been hoped would see the royals triumphantly and joyfully into the twenty-first century. It survived only eleven mostly miserable years; Diana herself claimed it was lucky to have survived the first.

Whether the break came in time to prevent lasting damage to the two boys, William and Harry, is still unknown, but tragically, by then, the boys were fully aware of their parents' problems and had been party to some of their most awful rows. What everyone—family, friends, courtiers and staff—agreed was that if there was not a radical change in their circumstances then the children would inevitably become emotionally scarred by the situation. It might already be too late. Wendy Berry had heard William, almost in tears, shouting at Charles, "I hate you, Papa. I hate you so much. Why do you make Mummy cry all the time?"

The official death-knell on the marriage was sounded by prime minister John Major on December 9, 1992. "It is announced from Buckingham Palace that, with regret, the Prince and Princess of Wales have decided to separate."

Hardly had the shockwaves from this announcement subsided and the New Year been welcomed in that a new blockbuster royal scandal exploded in the press. This time it was Diana's turn to grin and Charles and Camilla's turn to squirm. It would make the Squidgy Tape revelations seem almost innocent by comparison.

SIX

The excruciating embarrassment experienced by Prince Charles and Camilla Parker Bowles on publication of their secretly taped late-night chat was no more than any other couple would feel if a private lovers' exchange were transcribed and printed in a major national newspaper. But this was not just any other couple. This was the married heir to the throne of England and the wife of one of his closest friends, and their silly, slightly dirty and very explicit conversation showed that they were heavily involved in an adulterous relationship.

Charles admits he needs her several times a week, and suggests it would be much easier if he just lived inside her trousers. But when she proposes that he turn into a pair of her knickers, he comes up with the idea of becoming a Tampax. Their talk is mainly about love-making and when they will meet again, and Charles tells her, "Your great achievement is to love me." They then spend a couple of minutes telling each other "I love you" in the way lovers do when they want their partner to ring off first.

Charles was staying at the home of Anne, Duchess of Westminster, and Camilla was at home in the country on December 17, 1989, when their telephone conversation was recorded by the intelligence services. It was done just two weeks before the Squidgy Tape was made, and almost certainly by the same team. As before, the eleven-minute conversation was electronically cleaned before being rebroadcast to be picked up by an amateur radio buff. It was originally sold to an Australian publication before being passed to the *Sun* in London where it was guaranteed to have the greatest impact.

The most savage reaction was against Camilla Parker Bowles who received hate mail by the sack load and—after an extremely harrowing incident in a local supermarket where she was pelted with bread rolls by other shoppers—was forced to remain hidden in her home.

Diana, on the other hand, was delighted. Having suffered so recently from the Squidgy Tape, she could fully appreciate just how much anguish and misery her rival was going through. A woman with Camilla's sheltered upbringing was bound to suffer much more from the full attention of the press. Camilla was in a purgatory of her own making, and Diana reveled in her public humiliation and disgrace. In addition to this, Mrs. Parker Bowles was suffering dreadful guilt pangs from the equally devastating effect the publishing of the tape had had on her husband—who was besieged by the

press on a daily basis. Andrew managed to preserve his unruffled graciousness and charm, and
said nothing. Camilla remained stoical but was unable to cope in public and went to pieces, holed
up in her house. In four short weeks she lost
twenty-five pounds in weight and aged a decade.

Camilla could only reveal her true feelings to
one man—Prince Charles, whom she rightfully
reasoned was the person most desperately in need
of her reassurance and loving support. But she
feared to tell him so on the telephone, for if one
call could be bugged—the prince eventually learned
that the secret service had twenty-eight highly intimate and revealing telephone conversations between himself and Camilla—then they figured,
correctly, that they were still being monitored.
However, they dared not meet face-to-face in case
they were discovered by the press.

It was no consolation to either of them that
Stella Rimington, the head of MI5, had set up an
in-house investigation to identify the "rogue
agents" who had secretly leaked the "Camillagate"
tape. The results of her investigation were never
released, and a government inquiry launched by
prime minister John Major concluded a year later
that the intelligence services had been cleared of
spying on the royal parties. These results were, jus-
tifiably, met with virtually universal disbelief and
derision by members of parliament and the general public alike. Charles, Camilla and Diana rejected the statement, and believed that they were
still being spied upon.

Of the three of them, Diana now had the least
to lose. Free of Charles after, in her own words,
"twelve fucking diabolical years," she had rarely

been in higher spirits, and the "Camillagate" revelations, in fully confirming her stories of Charles's involvement with Mrs. Parker Bowles, which had been dismissed by most Establishment figures as paranoid hysteria, had made her ecstatically happy. There was a new bounce in her step, and a renewed sparkle in her brilliant blue eyes. Diana was at her best ever, and clearly planning to make the most of her hard-won freedom.

She was absolutely convinced now that she could fulfill all her potential as Princess of Wales, naively believing that her split with Charles had not affected her formal position in the royal hierarchy and that it would remain equally unaffected by divorce, which at that time she would not openly admit to being an option. It certainly did not exist in Diana's own somewhat blinkered version of her destiny. In her confused vision of the future, she would enjoy a solo role uncluttered by Prince Charles, all the while remaining married with her existing privileges intact. The confusion already existing in her mind was illustrated by her great joy at being free of Charles, which alternated with moments when she confided to friends that she still loved the prince as much as ever and still wanted her marriage to work.

For his part, Charles had little time to dwell on the future of his marriage. His future in history was being threatened by the public debates raging in the media and among churchmen and politicians following publication of the "Camillagate" tape. There had even been the most amazing backlash among his most ardent supporters in the Establishment. Those who had sympathized with the prince after the Squidgy Tape was released now stood back appalled, and even questioned his suitability to become king. Even his hard-core supporters were devastated.

In the first six days of March 1993, column inches in the British national press totalled 3,603 supporting Diana and just 275 for Charles. What frightened Charles's supporters most was his apparent inability to fight back, for once again the prince was showing weakness in the face of adversity. In the spring of 1993, his official visit to Mexico was completely overshadowed by Diana's five-day trip to Nepal, and at times it must have seemed to the beleaguered prince that the whole world was turning against him.

According to her personal protection officer at the time, Ken Wharfe, Diana went through a period of secretly hoping that the unthinkable would happen and the monarchy skip a generation—the crown bypassing Charles and going directly to Prince William. This scenario, Wharfe believed, agreed with her slightly twisted idea of justice.

Wharfe, and others close to the princess—who was now referred to by everyone as "the boss"—noticed a huge change in her following the separation. She had grown in confidence when coping with public events, but at the same time her confidence and trust in her inner circle of confidantes began to wane. It seemed that she felt she had been betrayed so many times in her life that it was becoming increasingly difficult for her to trust anyone. She became highly unpredictable, with spectacular mood swings, and it seemed to some of those in contact with her on a daily basis that she had grown a conviction that she was engaged in a personal witch hunt. She started to accuse those closest to her of treachery and deceit.

What Diana craved more than anything else at that time was to have a special place, a bolt-hole, call it what you will: somewhere she could call her own and hide when she felt vulnerable, free of neighbors, and even servants if she so chose, and out of the reach of the ever more intrusive camera lenses.

With little optimism—as they rarely communicated—she decided to ask her brother, Charles, if she could have the use of a property on the Spencer estate. He surprised her by offering her the use of Garden House, with its own swimming pool, and with a gardener and cleaner thrown in, for £12,000 a year. It was early in June that the earl wrote that he could see her need for a country retreat and was happy to help provide it. Diana was ecstatic, and while Ken Wharfe was checking out the security arrangements, she started talking to interior designers. But it was all a waste of time. Two weeks later, in a dispassionate letter, her brother wrote to tell her the whole deal was off. He was sorry, he wrote, but he just couldn't help her. The police and press interference would be too much and would be wrong for his wife and children.

The princess was devastated, and when Charles telephoned she refused to speak to him. She could barely accept that her own brother could be so cruel. It was the start of a rift between them which widened with time, becoming virtually beyond repair later that year when Earl Spencer demanded the return of the Spencer family tiara, which her

father had suggested she wear on her wedding day.
It was something she still wore on state occasions
such as the opening of parliament. It was time, he
wrote, to return it to its proper owner—himself.
His wife Victoria was the right person to wear it.
Diana lost a tiara; the earl lost the respect and love
of his sister.

Despite her enormous popularity rating among
the people, Diana was a lonely woman who
needed the reassurance and comfort that only a
lover could provide. Unfortunately for her, the
man with whom she was currently obsessed—
Diana's loves were always "all or nothing" affairs,
and she became besotted with each man with
whom she was involved—was still antiques dealer
Oliver Hoare. He was married and, although he
was understandably thrilled to continue a covert
sexual relationship with such a stunning mistress,
he had not the slightest intention of leaving his
wife for her.

His time spent with Diana making love, and
even the time he could spare to talk with her on
the telephone was severely limited by the demands
of his marriage and business. It was too limited for
a woman with a great deal of spare time on her
hands and a chronic need to be loved and constantly to be reassured. Diana was used to getting
her own way most of the time, and believed some
things to be hers by right. One of those things was
her right to speak to her lover whenever she
chose. This meant the Hoare home telephone in
Chelsea received dozens of calls every day and
every night. If they happened to be answered by
Diane Hoare, as was usually the case, the princess
would hang up.

Oliver Hoare begged his mistress to stop making the calls, and promised that he would call her at set arranged times each day and night—but this had no effect at all. As all men discovered when they entered into a relationship with Diana, they had to capitulate entirely to her terms. Hoare was no exception.

The calls continued unabated until October 1993 when Diane Hoare, in exasperation, called the police and made an official complaint. Over a short period over 400 calls were logged and all were found to be coming from individual private lines within Kensington Palace. Chelsea police contacted the head of the Royal Protection Squad, who in turn contacted Ken Wharfe. He told Wharfe it was believed the nuisance calls to Hoare's home were being made by a disgruntled member of the princess's staff.

An incredulous Ken Wharfe had to explain that it was the princess herself, and not her staff, who was making the calls. When confronted, an aggressive Diana admitted making some of the calls, but said she was not responsible for the majority. When the press, inevitably, got hold of the story, Diana felt she was being persecuted, explained Wharfe. She did not once show any remorse and did not seem to think she had done anything wrong. But having received a police warning, albeit with bad grace, Diana backed off and her obsession with Hoare began to cool.

Prince Charles and his supporters may have been privately delighted by Diana's embarrassment, but they were in no position to take advantage of her fleeting fall in the public's esteem. They were far too busy fighting off a concerted effort by some of the leading figures in the Church of England who questioned his very right to be king.

"Does he have the right to be trusted with the role of king, if his attitude toward matrimony is so cavalier?" asked the Archdeacon of York, the Venerable George Austin. "Prince Charles made solemn vows before God in church about his marriage, and it seems he began to break them immediately."

Other senior bishops joined in, including the Bishop of Sodor and Man, who declared that the breaking of the marriage vows was an "indication of a moral flaw which should be worrying, I think. I do not happily accept the remarriage of divorcees in church."

The Bishop of Kensington added, "To marry a divorcee would render his position untenable. If he were to marry a divorcee, he would have to renounce the crown."

Such a concerted attack on a member of the royal family by such important church leaders was unprecedented, and was immediately compounded by the results of a survey taken of 100 members of the 574-strong Church of England ruling body, the Synod, made up of bishops, clergy and laity. Forty-seven percent thought the prince, unlike any of his predecessors in the previous 400 years, should not become supreme governor of the Church of England upon his accession to the throne, while twenty-seven percent thought he should not even become king if it were shown to be true that he had had an affair with Camilla Parker Bowles.

The Church's reply to a Buckingham Palace–Downing Street assurance that the separation of Charles and Diana had no constitutional implications came through the former Bishop of Birmingham, the Right Reverend Hugh Montefiore: "The separated Princess of Wales cannot be crowned Queen. It would be abhorrent to a large proportion of the English people. The question is bound to arise whether the archbishop would in good conscience be able to crown her."

It was clear to anyone that Charles's popularity with the Church was at an all-time low and that his insistence on a divorce from Diana and a closer relationship with Mrs. Parker Bowles could make his position worse in the clergy's eyes. Complete celibacy and a total commitment to good works, rather than pleasurable pursuits, was the lifestyle now demanded by the church to improve Charles's tarnished image.

Courtiers at St. James's Palace felt powerless to intervene, and feared an even worse reaction from the Church if the divorce were to go through, as Charles fully intended. They blamed the media for many of Charles's woes; but above all they believed the real culprit to be Diana, and they loathed her for it.

Yet the more they tried to edge her out, the more she made them suffer. Her name was dropped from the royal family's star list, and that year Royal Ascot was one major event to which she was not invited. Instead, on that day, Diana took her sons to Planet Hollywood, and scooped the front pages. When her invite to the Queen Mother's birthday celebration did not arrive, she and the boys went go-carting. The front pages were all hers again. When the Queen made her first visit to a post-communist country—Hungary—Princess Diana went to Paris, shopping. It was no contest. What pictures of the Queen did appear were tucked away inside.

The front pages were dominated by her estranged daughter-in-law.

Charles never felt himself to blame. What he had done was what male members of the royal family had done for centuries. It was, he believed, his God-given right by virtue of his birth to commit adultery if it pleased him to do so. The rules had altered, and he could not accept the new order of things. He had no understanding of what had changed, which is why he felt no remorse or contrition—only anger and frustration.

One telling remark, shouted during one of their worst rows, reveals the prince's heartfelt exasperation best: "Do you expect me to be the first Prince of Wales in history not to have a mistress?" he challenged Diana.

In December, when Charles arrived on an official visit to Southwark, south London, only two members of the public turned out to see him—plus thirteen photographers and ten reporters. At the same time, Diana made a trip to Belfast—unannounced for security reasons—and attracted more than 150 people, thirty photographers and ten reporters. Diana had recently revealed, in an emotional announcement, that she would no longer undertake official public engagements. Belfast was one of the last.

For Charles, his wife's withdrawal from public duty could not come soon enough. The turnouts for his public appearances were pathetic, each one heaping further humiliation on top of humiliation, and when a tour of Australia was proposed he initially refused even to contemplate it. The

Australian prime minister had already committed his country to becoming a republic at some time in the future, and Charles felt that in the present circumstances he would be risking poor public relations. His advisers, however, were desperate to get some favorable press and, knowing that British journalists were kinder to their royal subjects on a foreign tour, insisted. In January 1994 the prince reluctantly began the Australian tour, although no one believed he could do much for his popularity figures either at home or in his host country.

Then a miracle occurred during the prince's first engagement at Tumbalong Park, Sydney. It came in the shape of a twenty-three-year-old anthropology student, David Kang, who pulled out a gun and ran toward Charles, who was on stage, firing into the air. The prince simply stood there, playing with his cufflinks, as Kang leaped to the stage, still firing his gun. Before the student could reach Charles, his foot caught in a cable and he fell heavily on the stage floor, where prize-winning guest Ian Kiernan, who had just been named Yachtsman of the Year, overpowered him.

Kang's gun had only contained blanks, and he was making a protest about the Cambodian boat people. The effect on his pet cause remains unknown, but the effect on Prince Charles's popularity rating in Australia was phenomenal. Recovering faster than anyone else, Charles had stepped to the microphone as Kang was dragged off stage and commented dryly, "It's alright for you, at least you've all had a drink."

Later at a press conference he glossed over the incident, saying that such alarms were all part of the job. His apparent bravery and casual rejection of any heroics mightily impressed the Australians who, two days later, turned out in the thousands to cheer their hero prince. A poll taken that day showed that sixty-six percent of Australians now believed him fit to be king and fifty-three percent believed he set a good example.

Back in England, as the year ran toward summer, there was little to cause excitement in either of the royal camps. Despite her decision to withdraw from public life—a decision forced upon her by the royal family behind the scenes and presented to the public as the princess's own wish—Diana was rarely out of the newspapers, even though she was only undertaking mundane tasks like shopping, dropping the boys at school, visiting the hairdresser or eating out at a restaurant. The demand for her was insatiable.

Charles maintained his public duties and gradually, as the interest died down, was able to renew his regular meetings with Camilla. His continuing concern was his popularity rating which, despite a slight lift after the Australian incident, again stood at an all-time low in Britain. But unknown to all but his most trusted courtiers and staff, Charles was working throughout that spring on a combined television documentary and biography with broadcaster Jonathan Dimbleby. Charles had been persuaded that cooperating in this venture, which would draw a line under his life to date and open the way for a new beginning, was a clever public relations gambit to boost his popularity. In reality, it was probably the worst PR decision he had made in his entire life.

In the television documentary, which was broadcast in the summer of 1994, Charles acknowledged his adultery with Camilla Parker Bowles. It was a serious miscalculation. The prince was not the first royal to be unfaithful, but he was the first to go on television and admit it to twenty million people. Nor was it clever of him to make it clear that he considered Diana to be little more than a hired womb.

The biography, *The Prince of Wales: A Biography*, followed in October. It certainly did not tell the truth about the prince's love affair with Camilla, maintaining that it was not until 1987, or even 1988, after Charles and Diana had begun leading separate lives, that he renewed his friendship with Camilla, and these meetings occurred mostly only when other people were present. Dimbleby, based on what Charles had told him, presents this partial truth of the affair as being the complete story and in this way the public was deflected from knowing the full extent of Charles's adultery.

One major repercussion of this ill-advised venture was the divorce of Andrew and Camilla Parker Bowles. They petitioned on the grounds that they had lived not more than ninety nights under the same roof in the previous three years. The twenty-one-year-old marriage took exactly three minutes to end in the High Court Family Division on January 19, 1995. The divorce did not improve Charles's popularity rating in the polls; nor did the world-exclusive story in the *News of the World* the following week in which Charles's valet of fifteen years, Ken Stromach, revealed that the prince and Camilla had systematically cheated on Diana for years, even making love at Highgrove when the princess was asleep in the marital bed.

"It is," said the paper's royal correspondent Clive

Goodman, "a story the Princess of Wales understands only too well—and it will cut her to the quick."

A photograph of Camilla at the Queen Mother's home, Birkhall, with Prince William in the background, was proof that the senior member of the royal family had condoned—and abetted—Charles's affair with Camilla, even while his sons were living under the same roof.

With these dual revelations, Diana had been given moral superiority by her husband and his mistress. She needed only to remain silent to retain this long-awaited advantage. But Diana wanted far more than the moral high ground. She wanted revenge, and there appeared to her to be only one satisfactory way for her to achieve it: by speaking out on television herself—and telling the public in her own words the horrors she had endured.

SEVEN

Rumors abounded that the Parker Bowleses' divorce was all part of a plot by Charles to renege on his destiny, like his great-uncle Edward VIII, and go into exile abroad with his paramour, leaving the throne when it became vacant to his son William. After his television confession of adultery, the public believed him capable of any slippery scheme to fulfill his well-publicized personal ambitions. Less than half the country thought he was fit to become king. Perhaps worse for the monarchy, many didn't seem to care one way or the other.

Instead of sitting back and enjoying the spectacle of Charles squirming to extricate himself from his self-committal to purgatory, Diana craved an opportunity to deliver the *coup de grâce* in person. Nothing else would quite satisfy in the same way.

Even after the publication of valet Stromach's revealing memoirs, which more than underscored Charles and Camilla's despicable treatment of her,

Diana was not convinced the public understood the full extent of his perfidy. Even so, she did not let these thoughts stop her from embarking upon another and this time highly unsuitable affair. The new man in her bed was the captain of the English rugby team, Will Carling, a boy's own hero, but also a newlywed.

Carling, scarcely back from his honeymoon with beautiful TV presenter Julia, had engineered a friendship with the princess's driver, Steve Davies, simply in order to set up a meeting with Diana at the Harbour Club, the exclusive gym in Chelsea where she worked out. Soon, devoted wife Julia was being fobbed off with weak excuses when she called trying to fix lunch dates with her husband. For three days a week he was at Kensington Palace reveling in a torrid love affair in Diana's bed.

Incredibly, Diana was able to juggle her love sessions with Will with her secret recording sessions with a BBC film crew; she had finally selected television as the medium for her exposé on her faithless husband and his mistress. She chose *Panorama* and BBC reporter Martin Bashir as her vehicle, and public confession as her weapon.

Throughout the program, broadcast in November 1995, she appeared to be on the verge of tears, and this impression was emphasized by her heavy eye makeup, dark clothes and the subdued lighting. Many of the takes were filmed several times, until the princess was satisfied with the effect, and her words, though delivered shakily, were clearly not the off-the-cuff responses suggested by the format, but carefully crafted statements. The whole interview was a masterly piece of theater, designed, with cleverly orchestrated pre-publicity, to wring the maximum sympathy and tears from the multi-million-strong viewing audience.

Two of her comments will particularly be remembered. That she doubted Charles was fit to be King, and that "there were three of us in this marriage, so it was a bit crowded."

If Diana's intention was to expose the full extent of her husband and Camilla's treachery and heap further contempt and loathing on them from an already disgusted public, then she succeeded brilliantly. But what she also did was to precipitate a divorce, and in a part of her heart Diana had always hoped that in some magical way Charles would one day tire of Camilla and return to live with her, "happily ever after" in true fairy-tale style. Her bravura television performance had ruled out that particular storybook ending and would no longer give her the opportunity to play the wronged wife.

What angered the men in the gray suits, however, was that Diana had developed the capability of outmaneuvering them.

Charles's supporters rallied around, led by Nicholas Soames, the grandson of Sir Winston Churchill, who accused Diana, in a television interview, of being in the advanced stages of paranoia, and said that the period of unhappiness which she had endured had led to instability and mental illness. Even her estranged brother apparently felt so distressed by Diana's behavior that he wrote her a letter, saying that he felt she had some kind of mental illness which manifested itself in her traits of manipulation and deceit. He acknowledges that she is no longer a significant part of his life, and says he prefers it that way because her fickle friendship had hurt so many others.

Diana expected comments on her mental state from the likes of Nicholas Soames, a Prince Charles toady, but not from her own brother. Their estrangement, already deeply rooted, grew several degrees more frosty. It would last until her murder, and must leave Earl Spencer with an awful burden of guilt.

Following Diana's *Panorama* appearance, the Queen called in the prime minister and the Archbishop of Canterbury for talks. These resulted in her writing separately to Charles and Diana ordering them to divorce. The princess had provided her palace enemies with a compelling reason to cut her loose. *Panorama* had condemned her to a future as an unsupported solo act.

Commented author A. N. Wilson in the *New York Times*, "No one can deny that this was a skillfully organized attack on the institution of the monarchy itself. Not just on Prince Charles, not just on the Queen, whom Diana obviously hates, but on the monarchy. The example of Wallis Simpson and Edward VIII should be enough to tell Diana that when it comes to fighting a war, the Establishment can get very nasty indeed, and that for all her undoubted popularity, if she continues to rock the boat in this way, the Establishment will simply get rid of her."

The financial cost to Charles was high—£17 million—but he was ordered by the Queen not to fight the princess on her payoff, no matter how unjust he felt it to be and no matter how angry he became. Diana's supporters always maintained that any one-on-one discussion about the divorce between Charles and Diana was very amicable. Charles's people tell a very different story. The prince told an aide he had been shocked by Diana's venom during their meetings. The aide said, "Charles said she told him, 'You will never be king. I shall destroy you.' "

Diana showed little inclination to argue terms, however. It was almost as though she had no follow-up plan and that *Panorama* had been an entity in itself. Diana did not seem to have fully anticipated the reaction and how she would handle it. The only bitterness she felt, and it was bitterness tempered with raw anger, was over the loss of her royal title. To take away her HRH was, she believed, a petty, mean and spiteful move on the part of the Queen. Ken Wharfe revealed that she believed that her years of hard work had earned her the title. She begged the royals not to take it away from her. Her appeals, through some of the top courtiers at the palace, including her brother-in-law Sir Robert Fellowes, the Queen's private secretary, were completely ignored.

It was such a shabby punishment, and even though delivered with a golden royal slipper, it was still a kick in the face for Diana. Staff and friends nodded when they heard her most frequently screamed cry, "After all I've fucking done for that family." This time every one of them agreed. Had she been allowed to keep her title, it may well have been the means of saving her life. As a visiting royal, the French authorities would have had no option but to protect her with a full security detail wherever she went—with or without her approval. Unlike her payoff price, though, it was not a subject for negotiation, she was told. There was absolutely no question of her being allowed to keep the title.

Until the eve of her divorce, she maintained to all and sundry that part of her still loved Charles and probably always would. But this version does not tally with that of some of her friends, with the recollections of Will Carling's wife Julia, nor with the family of the man with whom she was becoming increasingly involved, heart surgeon Dr. Hasnat Khan. To them all, it seemed that her craving for affection remained unabated.

The Carling affair had ended in the spring, after the cheating rugby star had confessed his adultery with the princess, and his wife sued for divorce. Diana had grown tired of Carling's puppy-like devotion, and she gave him the royal elbow—something at which she was becoming increasingly skilled. As a child she had learned to play one parent off against the other. In adult life, her friends, both men and women, never knew when they were going to be crossed off her list or for what reason. Suddenly her private number changed, she didn't answer their letters, and the Buckingham Palace general switchboard refused to connect them to her apartment at Kensington Palace.

If it was difficult for Diana's staff, friends and boyfriends to keep track of her bewildering turnover in men, then it was even more complicated for her son, Prince William, still only fourteen. Any young man of that age could have found it difficult to cope, but it seems he managed to—a testimony perhaps to his strength of character. It was the Queen who first realized the enormous strain that William was being subjected to by the princess, and it was she, characteristically, who stepped in to help. She was extremely concerned, she told her aides, and feared at one point that her grandson was at risk of "cracking up like his mother."

In her splendid biography of William, Ingrid Seward quotes Diana's close friend Rosa Monckton as saying that the princess "told Prince William more than most mothers would have told their children. She had no choice. She wanted her sons to hear the truth from her, about her life and the people she was seeing, and what they meant to her, rather than read a frequently untrue version in the tabloids."

The Queen's answer was to arrange a weekly meeting with the teenage prince to swap stories about each other's experiences over tea and buns at Windsor Castle, close to Eton College where William was a pupil. The Queen's advisers applauded her personal effort to reduce the pressures on her grandson, as did their opposite numbers in St. James's Palace, whose master, Prince Charles, seemed either less informed than his mother or less inclined to think the situation was causing damage to his eldest son.

The faceless men in the two palaces, however, were in no doubt that their future king was in extreme moral danger and being overloaded with the burden of acting as his mother's confessor.

Diana's confidant, Vivienne Parry, noted, "I'm not sure she was right to confide in him in that way. He was pretty level-headed but it must have been very difficult for him." No one genuinely believed there was anything terribly wrong with William having access to soft pornographic magazines, as this was considered a normal development in a western teenage boy's life. What was peculiar was that they were being ordered for him by his own mother, who instructed her staff what to buy. Diana believed that in doing so she was revealing herself as a modern, "cool" mum. But it was an extraordinary twist which few cared to speculate on with regard to its long-term effects.

In her dealings with Hasnat Khan, the princess had little to complain of to her son. There was no restriction put on Dr. Khan's access to Diana either by telephone or in person, and William and her friends could rejoice that she was with someone who was making her happy. Through most of that year they had enjoyed a secret but intense love affair, and her feelings for this new man in her life had already become so powerful and obsessive that she was seriously talking of marriage.

She had met Dr. Khan, a talented thirty-six-year-old cardiologist, while visiting a patient at the Brompton Hospital. He was chief assistant to Sir Magdi Yacoub—one of the world's greatest heart surgeons—and dedicated to his profession. An eligible, good-looking Pakistani, Dr. Khan tended to shun the limelight, and although he admitted falling in love with the princess, he had warned her from the start of their affair that he did not want it to become public knowledge. When they became lovers, Diana begged him to move in to Kensington Palace and live openly with her, but he was reluctant to acknowledge the seriousness of the affair and clung to his independence and privacy. To be close to the surgeon, Diana took to spending several nights a week at the Brompton Hospital, often accompanying Dr. Khan on his rounds before spending cramped nights of love on a single bed in the surgeon's on-call bedroom.

So besotted did Diana become that she made a special pilgrimage to Khan's home town in Pakistan to visit his parents and family in a bid to win their approval for marriage. Yet although they accepted her sincerity, the Khans advised her that it was their belief that Hasnat's future happiness was better assured if he married a member of their own Punjabi clan, the Pathons.

Diana dreamed up crazy escape plans where they could run away together, marry and live happily ever after with him being a surgeon and her being a loving housewife. When he told her it was madness and that it could never work, she would sob inconsolably. His mother said the princess became so desperate to marry Hasnat that she planned to convert to the Muslim faith. Nahid Khan said, "Everyone knew she wanted to marry him, but my son felt it would be impossible. He believed they would not be able to go anywhere together. Their cultures were so different."

She said Diana wrote letters full of love to the Khan family, but that Hasnat did not share the princess's enthusiasm for marriage. As 1996 came to a close, and more details of their affair leaked to the press, Dr. Khan became increasingly uncomfortable. His medical ambitions transcended everything—including Diana—and he was starting to find that their relationship was interfering with his work. He feared that marriage to Diana would quickly transform him into a celebrity, and was convinced this would in turn prevent him continuing with his life-saving medical career.

* * *

After the divorce, Charles tried hard to return to life as a single man. Priority was given to achieving the rehabilitation of Camilla Parker Bowles—at this point one of the most detested women in Britain—for even then he was determined that they would one day live together openly as man and wife. Commander Richard Aylard, the Prince's private secretary who had encouraged Charles to confess his adultery on television, was sacked, and Mark Bolland from the Press Complaints Committee was drafted to spearhead Camilla's re-imaging.

It was no easy undertaking as, following the divorce, a survey of Church members revealed that more than half believed Charles should become neither king nor head of the Church if he remarried. Charles's arrogant and near-contemptuous response to this was to issue a royal edict to all his staff that from that moment on, Mrs. Parker Bowles must be considered a nonnegotiable part of his life. It is a phrase still used by the Prince of Wales to this day whenever the subject of Camilla is raised. By the spring of 1997, Charles was openly living with his paramour at Highgrove and she rarely returned to her own house at Raybridge in Wiltshire.

Earlier in the year, Diana had decided to raise her game and, amid unprecedented publicity, launched her personal crusade, the emotional and passion-charged campaign to highlight the incredible cost of human life caused by anti-personnel land mines. It was a crusade that would embroil politicians of all persuasions and recruit government support at the highest levels, while incensing arms-trade profiteers and U.S. military chiefs.

In January, amid an unprecedented storm of international media attention, Diana arrived at the dilapidated Luanda Airport, close to Angola's capital and declared the start of her crusade to clean up the world. In the rubble that still surrounded the airport she spoke with raw passion of her commitment to banning anti-personnel land mines once and for all, and promised to force a cleanup program that would reduce further innocent slaughter. As queen of people's hearts, a humanitarian, she vowed to draw the world's attention to the forgotten victims of war, the innocents killed or maimed by taking a single wrong step in a flower-strewn meadow, former children's playground or ordinary village street.

In taking this step, Diana had carved out a dynamic new role for herself on the international stage. She had just as certainly ensured that Prince Charles's role would be diminished accordingly. The prince had once enlisted prime minister John Major's aid in his desire to stand alone on the royal stage. That was three years earlier, when Diana had fought back strongly, but lost. The palace, however, was no longer in a position to silence her or sidetrack her into the wings and obscurity. This time she meant to keep Charles out of the limelight for years.

The palace had made a classic mistake in forcing Diana to play second fiddle to the prince after their separation was suggested. It had only made her more determined to bounce back stronger when the right moment arrived. Freed by divorce from any obligation to the palace's authority, Diana had used the intervening year to increase her own popularity and come up with her personal crusade plan. The Queen of Hearts campaign could not have been bettered by any public relations expert in the world.

At the time of the princess's visit, 2,000 Angolans a month were losing limbs by stepping on uncleared land mines. Facts like this, and the sight of torn, blood-soaked bodies of children gathered into Diana's arms, created a powerful message. Diana not only forced debate into the forefront of the political arena by going to Angola—and later to Bosnia—but caused the Red Cross appeal takings to soar to £1,200,000 and counting.

The previous Red Cross land mines appeal had failed to raise £50,000.

By June, the princess was able to report personally to Hillary Clinton at a private meeting in the White House that her crusade was already showing staggering results. It was Hillary who had first suggested the land mines campaign to Diana, explaining that she, even as the president's wife, had achieved nothing for this issue. Diana told her of her plans for a trip to Bosnia, and the two women talked of Cambodia and Vietnam as being future countries to put under the campaign spotlight. Hillary Clinton insisted on her husband joining them to hear Diana's news for himself. He was still backing her land mines treaty, he told her.

It was at this stage that Diana's fate was effectively sealed. By the time it came for Bill Clinton to sign the treaty in Oslo in September, she would be dead, leaving the president free to renege on his promise—a move considered impossible while she was alive.

Sir Nicholas Bonsor, a former Foreign Office minister, told ITN, "For the princess to put herself so overtly at the head of a political campaign to abandon all land mines and deprive our soldiers of the use of such land mines was, in my view, wrong of her. I think it was dangerous for the royal family to have a member of its clan behaving in that kind of irresponsible fashion."

Diana gave her reply in a speech to the London Geographical Society on June 12, 1997. She attacked "these ghastly conservatives," as she called them, who had wrongly interpreted her visit to Angola as a political statement in favor of New Labour policy, and launched a full-scale attack on the arms trade. She vowed to continue her personal crusade and declared her utter refusal to let the issue drop. The Queen of Hearts stood squarely against the manufacture, sale and deployment of land mines.

By early summer, Diana's love affair was running a poor second to her land mines campaign. In fact it had run into serious trouble. Dr. Khan told the princess in May 1997 that he was unable to continue their relationship as he felt he was obliged to marry someone of his parents' choosing, as was Punjabi tradition. It was a tremendous blow to Diana, who had never before been dumped by a lover. She had offered marriage, to have his children, to change her religion to his and to learn his language, but all to no avail.

Hasnat Khan's rejection triggered a spate of outings with another Pakistani admirer, millionaire electronics company chief Gulu Lavani, a fifty-eight-year-old divorced father of three. But friends say this was only a ruse to get Hasnat Khan to change his mind. For a brief period she allowed Lavani to dine and dance her, but he fell far short of what she really needed, and he was soon sidelined to join her other discarded boyfriends. She had spent the last two years of her life hopping from bed to bed, desperately searching for love, to be included as part of a family, and yet she found herself once more alone. Worshipped by untold millions but loved, simply and with genuine affection, by no one.

It made Charles's announcement that he was throwing a ball at Highgrove to celebrate Camilla's fiftieth birthday on July 17 even more galling. It was something he had never done for Diana in all the time they were married.

Diana suddenly found herself almost completely isolated. The royal family had no time for her. The princes were welcome in Windsor, Sandringham and Balmoral, but not Diana. She was starved of family love. Her father was dead, and even he had been like a stranger toward the end. She and her brother Charles were still barely on speaking terms. His attack on her mental stability still rankled and she had not forgiven his refusal to grant her a hideaway at Althorp. His treatment generally, she felt, had been shabby since she had lost the HRH title, meaning that he was no longer allowed, even at secondhand, to rub shoulders with the royal family. Her mother, she considered, was more critic than comfort, and Frances Shand-Kydd and the princess had finally stopped talking to one another a month before Diana had been abandoned by Hasnat Khan after Mrs. Shand Kydd told her, in very slurred words, that she should change her choice in men and "stop going out with fucking niggers." "In just those words," Diana told friends. Her relationship with her sisters was not a great deal better. Jane was married to Sir Robert Fellowes, the Queen's private secretary, and was thus considered one of the enemy; and she and Sarah socialized less and less.

It seemed almost inevitable to Princess Diana that her next romance would be equally repugnant to her own family, the royal family and the faceless, gray-suited forces that unemotionally tended to the royals' unbidden orders.

She was right.

EIGHT

The romance between Princess Diana and the Oscar-winning playboy film producer Dodi Fayed began aboard Mohamed Al Fayed's £20 million yacht, *Jonikal*, which was moored in the harbor of Cannes in the south of France. Contrary to newspaper stories, Al Fayed had not invited Diana to holiday with his family. She had invited herself, and her two sons.

It was at a charity dinner during the winter of 1996 that the princess had asked him where he was going for his summer holidays. He told her he and his whole family would be going to St. Tropez where, apart from the villa in its eight-acre holiday compound, he had two magnificent yachts. Wistfully, she said, "I wish I could do something like that. I'll bet my boys would enjoy it. I know I would."

Al Fayed laughed and said, "So, why don't you come along? The more the merrier." To him it had been small talk, not an invitation, but three weeks before the Fayed family was scheduled to leave for their villa on the French Riviera, Princess Diana telephoned Mohamed at his office and said that she was very lonely and would like to go on holiday with his family and bring the two young princes.

When Al Fayed's private Gulfstream IV jet, painted in the distinctive green and gold livery of Harrods, took off from Gatwick to carry the Fayed family to Nice Airport, Princess Diana, Prince William and Prince Harry were with them.

Diana, the consummate media manipulator, knew exactly what she was doing when she picked Mohamed Al Fayed to be her holiday host and protector. The overtly benevolent Egyptian is the man the British Establishment least wants as a fellow citizen. The cash-for-parliamentary-questions protagonist who owns Harrods and wielded an unhealthy control in parliament, looked set to be forging an explosive new bond with the mother of the future king. From the moment Diana stepped aboard his private jet, intense speculation gripped the globe.

There was a history between them. Ten years before, Al Fayed had revived the Harrods polo competition at the Guards Club in Windsor Great Park where his team, led by his son Dodi, had beaten Charles's team. Mohamed Al Fayed had comforted Diana then. He had also been a good friend of Diana's father, and had kept a fatherly eye on the princess ever since the earl's death. Diana's once-hated stepmother, Raine, who latterly had become a close confidante and whose advice the princess had grown to value highly, was a director of Harrods.

What the world did not readily appreciate is

that Diana also enjoyed the raucous and earthy side of Al Fayed, and loved his wicked sense of humor. Now the man who arguably did as much as the Tories themselves to bring down the John Major government was host for ten days to the world's most exciting woman—and his son was speeding south by private jet from Paris. For a long time the Egyptian entrepreneur had entertained the idea that his son was destined to marry the Princess of Wales, and their meeting this time, Al Fayed was convinced, would produce the romance of the century.

Dodi Fayed, sometime film producer, sometime Harrods' apprentice boss, and then aged forty-one, reveled in fast cars and beautiful women and owned expensive homes all over the world. They included a dream mansion in Malibu, Los Angeles, apartments in London, Paris, the United Arab Emirates and New York, and the use of family estates in Gstaad, St. Tropez, Oxted in Surrey, a castle in Scotland and the Duke of Windsor's former house in the Bois de Boulogne, Paris. Add to this a flotilla of yachts, a Gulfstream IV jet, a fleet of cars—including Ferraris and a U.S. army armored truck—and a helicopter, and the picture of his truly opulent lifestyle begins to emerge.

Dodi's mother was Samira Khashoggi, the sister of the Middle Eastern multimillionaire arms dealer Adnan Khashoggi, and he had finished his education at the officer-training college Sandhurst. Dodi had been briefly married to, and divorced from, a model in 1986, and his name had been linked with numerous beauties. These included Brooke Shields, Princess Stephanie of Monaco, Tina Sinatra, Tanya Roberts and Patsy Kensit.

His allowance from his father at the time was set at £7.5 million a year—or £145,000 a week.

According to his father, Dodi did not even know the princess was in the family complex at St. Tropez until he called him in Paris. He was busy making love to a beautiful California model, Kelly Fisher, in his sumptuous Paris apartment off the Champs Elysées, and planning a party with friends to celebrate Bastille Day. But July 14 brought the urgent summons from his father that Princess Diana needed an escort and companion and Dodi, with Kelly Fisher still in tow, dashed immediately for Le Bourget airport where his pilots had already filed a flight plan for Nice.

Dodi had left behind his friends to celebrate Bastille Day without him, but Al Fayed promised him better entertainment. He would take his holiday party on his £20 million yacht, the *Jonikal*, to Cannes, and would rendezvous there with Dodi for the town's annual Bastille Day fireworks.

Dodi's own yacht, a converted motor torpedo boat, the *Cujo*, was moored along the coast and he reached Cannes harbor minutes before the *Jonikal*— 195 feet in length, sleek, white and as impressive as anything that night afloat in the billionaires' hangout—made fast its mooring ropes. Dodi immediately transferred to his father's boat, leaving Kelly Fisher aboard the *Cujo*. The model later claimed Dodi had proposed to her and given her an expensive engagement ring, but when Dodi met Diana, friends say, it was obvious to anyone watching that all other bets were off. Dodi abandoned the yacht next day when they returned to St. Tropez, and moved into the villa. Kelly Fisher was to see very little of him during the following week.

Friends remember that, from the moment Diana and Dodi met, they had eyes only for each other. The day after he joined her, Diana's good friend, designer Gianni Versace, was killed, and Dodi was able to provide a more-than-comforting shoulder to cry on. They quickly discovered that they liked each other, and that rapidly, that liking became something considerably deeper.

"Dodi was very laid-back," said one friend. "One could truthfully say about him that he strolled through life. There was nothing pushy or aggressive in his approach to women. It was an approach bound to appeal to someone of Diana's wary celebrity."

Dodi was rich, well mannered and attentive and she could not help recognizing how favorably he compared to most of the previous men in her life. On top of this, she told a friend, "He is one of the few people in my life who wants nothing from me but my own happiness."

The *Mirror* quoted another friend who revealed that Diana had admitted, "I trust him. I think he can provide absolutely everything I need."

For Diana there was also the added pleasure of annoying the despised Establishment by fully embracing Mohamed Al Fayed and his family. More than that, she actually confided in them some of her most precious secrets. During her holiday, Diana talked openly to her hosts of her fears for her safety, and of the secrets she had locked away as insurance against assassination, said Mohamed Al Fayed. That the princess would willingly confide in the man who had personally wrecked the careers of Neil Hamilton and Jonathan Aitken and destroyed the Conservative government, left palace courtiers aghast.

Mohamed Al Fayed later revealed what she had confided in them. "This was not play-acting. She was genuinely concerned that there were powerful people at court who meant to harm her. Who were determined to arrange her death and make it look an accident. She was very upset, and in tears, when she told us, and sobbed that she lived in the constant fear that the nightmare world of paid assassins was all set to engulf her. She even warned Dodi that she strongly believed that anyone who became too close to her would also find himself in danger. Dodi tried to brush it off with a light remark but she told him to treat the threat seriously. 'People who get close to me are in mortal danger,' she warned."

But most of her time with them was very happy, he said. She told him and his wife Heini that this was the best holiday of her life. It would be hell going back to England and having to hand over the two princes to their father to join the royal family for their traditional Balmoral summer holiday. "She didn't know that after that she was destined never to see them again," he said.

On the day of Camilla's birthday party, Diana made quite sure which photographs would swamp the front pages. They were of herself in a purple swimsuit, looking absolutely ravishing and relaxed, playing with her boys and with Dodi's arm around her waist. Mohamed Al Fayed, in matching purple trunks, provided comic relief. Other pictures showed the couple cavorting on the boat and in the sea, and no one at the time could remember any set of photographs that had caught Diana in a happier mood. One could not imagine anything more different from the pictures which had been taken during her loveless fifteen-year marriage to Charles. For someone whose life had lacked fun and love for so long, the future was suddenly looking decidedly more rose-tinted, and Diana seemed determined to enjoy it. In one bizarre incident, she sailed close to the launch carrying the British royal press corps—the *créme de la scum* as they are known—and told them, "You are going to get a big surprise at the next thing I do."

Diana told close friends that Dodi showered her with love and expensive gifts. "He's so wonderful," she confided. "He doesn't need to give me expensive things. I'd willingly give myself to him for nothing." Probably for the first time in her life, Diana was being treated like a princess. Had she finally found the love that she craved since childhood? The two princes were certainly impressed. They approved of Dodi's visits to the local fun fair and his booking a local disco exclusively for them and the Fayed family. They liked the fact that he assumed the boys would stay up to participate in and enjoy it—which they did.

Diana should have returned to London on July 18, but stayed on a couple of extra days because she was so happy. Back in England, looking tanned and relaxed and unrecognizable from the pale, tearful figure of a year earlier, Diana told her stepmother Raine Spencer, "It was the best family holiday I've ever had."

"She told me she had met someone special," said Raine. "Someone who liked her for who, rather than what, she was."

After Diana left on July 20, Dodi rejoined Kelly Fisher, who had been abandoned aboard the *Cujo* throughout the princess's holiday, and two days later he flew with the bemused American to Paris, where she learned that her days of flying by private jet were over. Kelly was allowed to keep her ring, but the next day she was given a first-class one-way ticket back to Los Angeles. She threw a press conference, bad-mouthing Dodi and warning Princess Diana against trusting her playboy ex-boyfriend, thus earning herself a footnote in British royal history.

Having dropped Kelly, Dodi flew to London. Diana had also returned there after attending Versace's funeral in Milan. How bizarre it was that, less than six weeks later, Diana would be murdered dressed from head to toe in clothes made for her by the late Gianni. As soon as she was back, Dodi invited the princess on their first real date, a secret tryst. That evening the Harrods helicopter whisked them to Paris where they had dinner before retiring to the most lavish and regal suite at the Ritz Hotel (owned by his father)—the £6,000-a-night Imperial Suite.

Dodi told Al Fayed that it was here, in the main bedroom decorated in a fusion of Egyptian and Empire styles, in a vast copy of Marie Antoinette's bed at Versailles, gilded and canopied in ivory and green silk, that they first slept together. He marked the occasion by giving her a fabulous gold watch, surrounded by diamonds.

Back in London, after their brief trip to Paris, Diana spent virtually every free moment with Dodi at his apartment in London's Park Lane or at Kensington Palace. When photographed arriving at his home, Diana walked in without a care who saw her. She seemed to be telling the world that her romance was for real and that she had nothing to hide. Dodi had their meals brought in on silver trays from the nearby Harry's Bar.

When she was informed by a courtier that Prince Charles was expressing concern about the effect the new man in her life might be causing on their two sons, Diana said his worries were laughable in view of his own undisguised affection for a woman other than their mother. So rapidly was the love affair developing that Diana didn't hesitate when Dodi suggested they fly down to join the *Jonikal* on August 1 and cruise some of the Mediterranean islands. She ignored criticism which followed her earlier holiday with the Fayed family, described as "irresponsible," "unwise" and "controversial," and told him she couldn't wait to return to the yacht which she had found as sumptuous as the Royal Yacht *Britannia*, with swimming pool, gymnasium, saunas and Jacuzzis, and run superbly by a crew of eighteen. It had the style and luxury of a five-star hotel. The salon had six large sofas and still seemed spacious.

Despite occasional pestering by paparazzi photographers, the couple were able to laze aboard or swim off secluded beaches during their island-hopping cruise. They visited Corsica and Sardinia before flying back to London together in the Al Fayed jet.

The suave heir to Al Fayed's vast fortune would make Diana an ideal husband, announced blonde Sky News presenter Tania Bryer, who had dated Dodi in the past. "He is warm and gentle. Not an aggressive macho sort. I can see why he appeals to

Diana," she said. "He is absolutely charming and one of the most genuine people you could meet." Diana seemed to have come to the same conclusion. She was unconcerned about this latest scrutiny of her private life, and told friends, "I am in good hands." A confidante of Diana was quoted at the time as saying, "Her friends are in no doubt that the princess is in love. It is the real thing."

There was real sexual chemistry between them, said one journalist when shown intimate photographs of the couple taken aboard the *Jonikal*. "They are oblivious to everyone and everything around them!"

One of the photographs to which he was referring—of the bikini-clad princess kissing Dodi on the deck of the *Jonikal*—was splashed all over the front page of the *Mirror*. Editor Piers Morgan had bought it on a one-day-exclusive basis from an Italian paparazzi photographer who had staked out the yacht. The following day the picture was bought by other national newspapers and given similar treatment. It made the photographer more than £1 million—an indication of the incredible interest in their romance at the time. Publication of the grainy photographs did not cause the princess's smile to dim by even a fraction. Uncharacteristically, she didn't appear to give a damn that her privacy had been invaded. There was almost a sense of relief that the romance was right out in the open. Their caress was a world away from Diana's rigid embraces with Prince Charles. There was no pretense, no guile; just a very genuine passion and sexuality which proved her feelings for Dodi better than any words might have done.

Some friends believed she might be contemplating a Jackie Kennedy-style marriage. Jackie married Aristotle Onassis because it gave her financial and physical security. In the palace, the comments continued to focus on her "bad judgment" in her choice of friends, and on Dodi being an unsuitable escort for the mother of the future king. The slightest suggestion of marriage between the princess and the son of Mohamed Al Fayed sent shudders of revulsion through the ranks of palace courtiers. They were not impressed by the remark of Dodi's friend, who said, "With him, Diana can have everything the royal family gave her—without having the annoyance of the royal family."

Said Raine Spencer, "I get very upset when people try to dismiss it as 'the summer romance'. That is understating the depth of the happiness they found together, the depth of their need for each other and the depth of a tremendous friendship, because that is all part of a love affair. All I know is that she was tremendously happy and very much in love."

On August 8, Diana was photographed leaving Dodi's apartment next door to the Dorchester Hotel at one o'clock in the morning, even though only hours later she was flying, in her new persona as Queen of Hearts, to Bosnia to publicize her fight against the use of land mines. She had not only become a troublesome stone in the shoe of the royal family, she was already considered a serious menace by large sections of the international armaments industry, and her visit to Bosnia was dramatically to step up her threat to their billions in profits.

Radiant, and looking like a love-struck teenager, Princess Diana was greeted by over sixty cameramen when she arrived in war-scarred Bosnia. This beautiful woman, who just couldn't stop smiling, was able, with scarcely an effort, to focus the world's attention on the horror of land mines. She wanted to show that the human misery caused by land mines was not confined to the developing world, but affected many thousands in Europe too. Most Bosnian mines remained unmapped, and the casualty rate was increasing as refugees returned to their abandoned homes which had been part of the battlefield.

For three days she talked to surviving victims of uncleared mines: men, women and children who had lost arms, legs or sight. Some of the children were so recently maimed that their entrails were still exposed. She hugged them as they died, and let her tears mingle with theirs and they—and the whole world—adored her. Pictures of her visit, which appeared in newspapers around the globe, encouraged people to put pressure on their leaders to support a ban on land mines. And the world leaders, including Bill Clinton, responded by confirming their intention to make such a ban unanimous.

One newspaper referred to her as "Mother Teresa with a crown," and experienced opinionmakers were staggered that this not-very-eloquent woman had become the most influential single personality in the world. The response to her simple appeal was unprecedented.

In the Pentagon in Washington, and among some of America's wealthiest arms dealers, it began to dawn on people that the Princess of Wales had not only become the most visible and intractable opponent of their policies, but she now represented the most serious current threat to their agendas. Former British government minister Lord Howe described her as "a loose cannon."

Given Diana's strong personal influence on American president Bill Clinton, and the added pressure which his wife Hillary, a committed devotee to the princess's campaign, could exert on him, it would have become clear, a former intelligence officer told me, that there was little chance of opponents to the land mines ban persuading him to change his mind while she remained able to keep him in line. "Getting rid of Diana was becoming their only viable option," he said.

While Diana was devoting all her energies, temporarily, to her Queen of Hearts campaign, Dodi took the opportunity to fly to Los Angeles to supervise construction of the house he was building in Paradise Cove, Malibu. The £4.5 million mansion stood in five acres of tropical gardens and had a superb private beach. From photographs he had shown her, Diana had already specifically suggested alterations he might make. To his great delight she had suggested they make the Paradise Cove home their major residence. She would retain Kensington Palace as a base for her official charity work, but she preferred to be based in America. She had already advised key staff they would be moving to California, she told him. (Early in 2004, Diana's close confidante and friend, dream analyst Joan Hanger, confirmed the princess's plans. She said that on a visit to Kensington Palace, Diana spoke to her of moving to live in Los Angeles where Dodi had a house. "She sparkled when she spoke about Dodi," said Miss Hanger.)

Dodi was thrilled to pass on her ideas to the

builders. She wanted to live with him there, and he was eager to make his home as attractive and as comfortable as possible for her. Diana genuinely appreciated good design. She had no real education, having left private school with few qualifications, but she did have an instinctive feel for design—a talent about which Prince Charles used to scoff.

Reunited after their brief separation, Diana and Dodi stuck to each other like superglue. If she didn't spend the night at Dodi's apartment, he slept at Kensington Palace. That they were inseparable did not prevent "friends" and servants trying to pry them apart. One of the people who did not like Dodi was Diana's so-called "rock," Paul Burrell. Nodding toward the closed door, behind which Dodi was sleeping, he peevishly told a visitor to Kensington Palace, "You know he isn't right for her, don't you?"

Strangely enough, when Burrell boasts he was spending nights sitting on the stairs discussing Dodi with the princess as her equal, and advising her on whether she should accept Fayed's proposal of marriage, the butler was not actually being spoken to by Diana, according to a fellow servant. He had been discovered, yet again, nosing through Diana's private correspondence, and had been given the silent treatment, one of the princess's favored punishments for troublesome staff. Diana's former housekeeper, Wendy Berry, recalled that at a staff lunch in San Lorenzo at the end of April, Paul Burrell had seemed on edge and had whispered conspiratorially to her that the princess wasn't speaking to him any more.

One reason that has been suggested why Burrell did not approve of Dodi Fayed, is because the gossip-gathering servant, so full of his own self-importance, felt unfairly treated. Dodi never included Burrell in the invitations extended to the princess. The Fayeds had servants aplenty, and believed Burrell to be superfluous to their requirements. Nor did Diana ever ask that he be allowed to accompany her, making somewhat suspect his claims about his indispensability and her utter reliance on him. Said Darren McGrady, "Paul thought he was above being a butler. He had what the Queen Mum used to call 'red-carpet fever'. He thought he was more important than he was."

What is clear is that Princess Diana clearly believed Dodi was very much the right man for her. After the kiss pictures were published, Dodi had flown in his butler of six years, René Delorme, from Paris to look after them in his London home and at the Fayed complex in Oxted, Surrey, where he arranged caviar and candlelit dinners in the gardens. On one trip to Oxted by helicopter, Dodi organized a secret visit to Derbyshire to meet Diana's psychic, Rita Rogers. The visit was important only because it was the first time Diana had ever introduced a man to one of her secret inner circle of valued spiritual advisers, and was a further pointer to how attached they had become.

On August 15, Diana flew to Greece for a cruise with her good friend Rosa Monckton, and borrowed Dodi's father's private Gulfstream IV jet to take them there. Dodi, meanwhile, made another lightning visit to Los Angeles. Both were back in London on August 21. Diana flew back from Greece to Stansted airport in the Al Fayed jet, and transferred to Battersea Heliport in Dodi's helicopter. From there she dashed to Kensington

Palace, allowing only enough time to freshen up before returning to Battersea with Dodi to helicopter back to Stansted and the refueled Gulfstream, which would fly them to the *Jonikal* for yet another holiday together on the Côte d'Azur. From Nice airport the couple were whisked by car and tender to where the *Jonikal* awaited them offshore at St. Laurent-de-Var, and while they relaxed in the master stateroom, which stretched the yacht's full width, the captain, Luigi del Tevere, motored south toward St. Tropez where they dropped anchor at 2 A.M.

Early the next morning they headed to Pamplona Bay where Dodi and Diana joined Mohamed Al Fayed and his wife and four children for a late lunch. By the time they left, late that afternoon, the *Jonikal* was being tailed by a small flotilla of press boats.

Once again the presence of paparazzi didn't appear to faze Diana in the slightest. The next morning, as became their pattern, Diana was up and about long before Dodi. Bodyguard Trevor Rees-Jones remembers she looked stunning in her bathing suit and made no effort to hide from photographers.

By late afternoon they were anchored off St. Jean Cap Ferrat, from where Dodi had planned to take Diana shopping and sightseeing in nearby Monaco. During their trip ashore, Dodi's butler René says they gave their bodyguards the slip while they toured the chic part of Monte Carlo and popped into Alberto Repossi, Dodi's favorite jewelery store in the prestigious Hermitage Hotel. The bodyguards, laughed Dodi, couldn't admit they had mislaid their charges, because to have done so would have constituted a sackable offence in the

Al Fayed code. In his book, Trevor Rees-Jones denies a visit was made to Repossi's, even though Mohamed Al Fayed obtained the CCTV film of the couple actually in the store. Ultimately it doesn't matter either way: the ring, which Dodi would collect from the jeweler's Paris branch a week later, was real enough.

The following day, off Portofino in Italy, the young lovers chose to stay aboard as the paparazzi were visible in force on shore. It did not appear to create any hardship for the pair who, the *Jonikal*'s crew noted, showed no embarrassment about being seen kissing and cuddling during their sunbathing sessions on deck. Their intimate display of affection aboard their personal love boat didn't stop even when they knew they were in full sight of photographers. "It was amazing," said paparazzo Jason Fraser. "Diana just let go."

Photographers in their small boats shadowed them to Porto Venere, to Elba and finally to the tiny island of Molara off Sardinia where, with excellent security planning, they managed to enjoy a spectacular beach barbecue away from the prying camera lenses. But by August 26, the paparazzi had brought in helicopters to buzz the yacht periodically and keep closer tabs on their targets.

By Friday, August 29, they were anchored off Cala di Volpe, a private Sardinian resort, where they were able to slip ashore virtually unmolested. But the paparazzi attention was becoming oppressive and the couple decided it was time to move on. The decision to fly to Paris was made early that evening, and a flight plan filed from Sardinia's Olbia Airport for the following day. Staff were told they would be spending only twenty-four hours in Paris before going on to London.

When the Ritz Hotel was advised from the Fayed London nerve center that Dodi and the princess would be arriving in Paris on Saturday, a copy of the memo went to acting head of security Henri Paul. He immediately canceled a planned weekend away with friends and put himself back on the rota to be personally in charge of the airport reception, and involved in the day's activities.

The main purpose in going to Paris, Dodi told the Harrods operations center in London, was to pick up a ring. Dodi would tell his step-uncle, Hussein Yassin, a former press attaché at the Saudi Embassy in Washington, who was staying in the Ritz that weekend, "Diana and I are getting married. You'll know about it officially very soon." Hussein's niece, Joumana, who was also in Paris, received a similar call that Saturday evening. Dodi told her, "Our marriage will be founded on true love."

A formal announcement would be made, Dodi told them, after the princess had broken the news to her two sons when they were reunited the following day. It was already decided that the ring he was collecting from Repossi, in the Place Vendôme, would be her engagement ring.

By the time the green and gold Gulfstream IV jet put down at Le Bourget airport in the northern suburbs of Paris at 3:22 P.M., Diana was as confident as she would ever be that she was truly in love, and ready for the whole world to know it. When their door opened onto the area reserved for private aircraft, the contrast with the Côte d'Azur could not have been greater. There was not the slightest breath of wind and the temperature was already soaring into the eighties.

The British Embassy had not been informed that Princess Diana was arriving, but waiting by the runway, unbidden, but provided by a thoughtful government, were the motorcycle outriders and black cars of the French diplomatic protection squad—the *Service de Protection des Hautes Personnalités* (SPHP). Ordinarily, the princess would have been entitled to a phalanx of police cars and motorcycle outriders, and protocol would have made it impossible for her to dispense with their services. But Diana had made her feelings absolutely clear to her young Egyptian boyfriend. Dodi Fayed was a mild, gentle man. But that morning he angrily waved away the protection party, telling them he was quite certain that his own bodyguards could adequately cover the safety of the princess.

In this he was, of course, mistaken. The SPHP was a collection of professional, highly trained and tough-as-old-boots police officers used to ferrying visiting foreign VIPs around Paris both discreetly and safely; they were ruthlessly efficient in their dealings with the paparazzi. They would have guaranteed Diana freedom from harassment by the photographers. A cohort of paparazzi, some no doubt alerted by colleagues in the south of France and others possibly by Al Fayed's people or a special tip-off, was already waiting at Le Bourget to picture them deplaning.

Yet even with the problem already confronting them, Dodi, fully supported by Diana, turned down a final SPHP offer of assistance and waved away the special security car sent for their use. Diana's fear of official security staff far outweighed her dislike of the paparazzi, whose chosen transport here, she would quickly learn, was motorcycles and scooters, and whose persistence and aggression would make the antics of their Mediterranean cousins seem almost friendly in comparison.

PART TWO

THE MURDER

NINE

Dodi was a divorced Muslim playboy who had enjoyed casual love affairs with a score or more famous actresses and models. His father was an Establishment-unfriendly billionaire who had bought his way into British society, had serious question marks over the source of his wealth and was brother-in-law to the world's biggest arms dealer. Every aspect of the relationship between Dodi, Mohamed Al Fayed and Princess Diana was alarming and, just one year after the divorce, the "loose cannon" seemed primed to explode.

One who appeared to see it coming was Prince Edward. When he was told she had been killed, he said, "It was the only way it was going to end. It was amazing it took that long for it to happen."

To the horrified members of the Establishment who saw the growing probability of marriage to the Egyptian playboy, prompting Diana's conversion to Islam, and the birth of a brown-skinned,

Muslim half-brother or sister for the future King William, the unfolding scenario was totally unacceptable. Rumors already abounded that the princess was pregnant—rumors that were given greater credence after her murder by the illegal violation of her body, carried out in secret in Paris under the guise of embalming. Word in Paris is that a senior secretary in Charles's office gave the go-ahead, which was passed on by Sir Michael Jay, the British ambassador; but whoever did give the French doctors their orders that day must have believed the rumors, otherwise why order the mini-embalming? The only possible reason was to muddy the waters of pregnancy speculation with formaldehyde.

Paris police commander Jean-Claude Mules, the man who signed Diana's death certificate, says the decision to embalm a part of Diana's body was made by a higher authority than himself. "Top police inspectors do not know about these things that take place at the diplomatic level," he said. No one on the French side thought to question if it was Diana's next of kin giving the orders. Prince Charles, remember, was not even related to her after their divorce. Her true next of kin were her mother and Prince William.

Confirmation that the princess was pregnant would have meant the racist element condemning her for producing a mixed-race child. The more liberal would have been supportive. Each faction would have had differing advice for William and Harry: to reject their mother's half-caste baby, or welcome it into the family with open arms.

Former MI6 officer Richard Tomlinson revealed that during his time with the British intelligence service he learned that there was unofficial but direct contact between certain senior and influential MI6 officers and senior members of the royal household, including those who practiced their dark arts in St. James's Palace and its twin palace of Buckingham. Many of these men share an Oxbridge background and continue to intermingle throughout their lives. They would have been told about any CIA operation against Diana and would have supported further MI6 involvement, said Tomlinson, who worked for British intelligence for five-and-a-half years.

Tomlinson was arrested at gunpoint and beaten up by DST (*Direction de la Surveillance du Territoire*— the French secret service) agents. He suffered a broken rib before being interrogated for eighteen hours at DST headquarters in Paris, to deter him giving this, and other important evidence, to Judge Hervé Stephan, the French magistrate in charge of the official inquiry into Diana's death. But he did appear before Stephan, and told him, "As long as they can get away with doing something then that's their only limit about what they will do. This includes assassination."

Tomlinson's conclusions are supported by former MI5 officer David Shayler, who says he is also convinced that MI6 is implicated in the crash. "There is compelling evidence to indicate that an intelligence service was involved in the crash," he told the *Daily Mail*. "Where evidence exists, it also points to MI6."

The princess's decision to embrace Islam could easily have affected relations between Church and state; in Israel, it was widely believed the union of Diana and Dodi signaled a change in world opinion in favor of the Arabs and consequently against Israeli interests. This concerned politicians on Capitol Hill as much as those in the Knesset.

Charles's supporters had also reacted badly to the latest pronouncement from the Church that the prince's divorce from Diana should not encourage a belief that he could ever win support or sympathy for a marriage to Camilla Parker Bowles. The only possible way that Charles could remarry legitimately—and still become king—was if Diana died and made him a widower in the eyes of the Church. Diana, however, was alive, and committed to upstaging Charles, as heir or king, for the rest of his life. There was no doubt in anyone's mind about her continuing need for revenge, nor that it would get progressively more demanding. There was no doubt either that on the death of the Queen, Diana would become the natural figurehead of the royal family and would not hesitate to take what she would assume to be her rightful place.

Could anyone seriously believe that Camilla would be capable of repelling a determined coup by Diana when her son became king-in-waiting, and that, backed by the Al Fayed millions, she could not have set up a glamorous court successfully to rival that of her ex-husband? Neither could those with Charles's welfare in mind forget that chilling promise the princess had made to him at the time of their divorce: "You will never be king. I will destroy you."

Judging by their track record, the Establishment was prepared to go to any lengths to protect the prince, and to promote any grotesque fiction to win their master a more sympathetic press, even to the extent of willfully launching a vicious, and wholly fictitious, attack on his own youngest brother, Edward, merely to provide a new focus for hostile public attention. "He was thrown to the tabloids as certainly as any Caesar threw adversaries to the lions—particularly his relatives," said one palace observer.

It followed Prince William's first day at St. Andrew's University. The press had agreed to leave William alone after that day, and *Ardent*, Prince Edward's film-production company, was a party to that agreement. Then stories appeared in the tabloids that Edward had personally sent in a secret camera crew to spy on his nephew and sneak candid shots of the student prince from a basement peephole on campus, for use in a royal documentary destined to be sold to American television. The whole nation was appalled at this shabby betrayal, more so because it involved the treachery of a not-very-popular uncle against an adored nephew. Edward's behavior was denounced as monstrous and deceitful, with colorful quotes provided by Charles's aides, who claimed the prince was incandescent with rage. "He was alleged by his aides to have berated his brother in a thundering phone call," said royal biographer and leading royal expert, Ingrid Seward. "Why was his son's privacy being invaded by a member of his own family?"

One tabloid produced a giant, front-page headline quote from Charles to Edward, F*** YOU, which had been leaked to the papers by the prince's aides along with all the other quotes allegedly used during the supposed family rows.

Not unnaturally, William was extremely angered, but also confused, by the press reports. While believing the stories about his uncle emanating from St. James's Palace, William was, at the same time, suspicious that he was being used by people close to his father to get at Edward, says Ingrid Seward. His skepticism turned out to be well founded, for the stories were lies, supporting a scenario dreamed up inside the palace to humiliate Edward and cut short his film career, of which the dark forces and the royal family in general, disapproved. They were also aimed at deflecting public attention away from Charles and Camilla on to a new villain among the royals. Even when he realized what damaging nonsense was being perpetrated in his name, the prince had gone along with the whole, disgusting charade.

When Edward sent copies of everything his company had filmed, together with their diaries and schedules, to Buckingham Palace, it was discovered that the only shots *Ardent* had taken of William were on his first day of term—no more than all the other television and film cameramen. And on a day it was claimed they had been secretly filming William from a spy center on the university campus, they proved they were all sixty miles away on a different location.

The scandal, including the detailed dialogue from family rows which had been leaked to the newspapers and television over a week, had been invented by Charles's aides to provide a new royal object of derision for the media. More importantly, far from exposing the truth and protecting his youngest brother's good name and reputation, Charles had taken advantage of the attack on Edward to cause him maximum damage. The whole sorry episode only seemed to prove that a lack of honesty and decency was a common psychosis among the dark forces within the twin palaces. An ambition to rid themselves, once and for all, of the problem of Princess Diana, fitted very comfortably into this psychosis.

I was told by the former European head of a major foreign intelligence organization that MI6 was already committed, under existing arrangements with the CIA, to support any action the Americans chose to initiate. The St. James's Palace and Buckingham Palace forces, opposed to the princess, would have been advised by their MI6 colleagues that strong support for cooperation with the CIA in arranging a solution would simply be an extension of existing house policy, said Richard Tomlinson, who was fired in 1995 when he announced he was writing a book about MI6. He was sent to prison for Official Secrets Act violations.

The whole operation would have been made a good deal easier when MI6 discovered they had one man who was very close to Dodi Fayed on its payroll, he said. "The acting chief of security at the Ritz Hotel, Henri Paul, had been working for the British secret service for years," revealed Tomlinson. "I came across his personal file when I was working for them in 1993. Henri Paul was a long-standing agent. But Judge Stephan didn't show the slightest interest in investigating his activities with MI6."

Stephan was reflecting the attitude of the Paris police, who, after conveniently concluding at the very outset of inquiries that Diana had died in an accident, simply refused to consider any other possibilities. Six years after the crash, Commander Mules told *News of the World* royal editor Clive Goodman, "If you start off with an investigation into an accident, one cannot add things that would only complicate the original hypothesis. As the crime squad we have an extremely precise and rigorous method of working. We put forward a theory and we prove it with the elements which confirm it."

Mules knew of Henri Paul's links with MI6 but ordered his men not to investigate. His excuse? "Secrets are secret, so we never could have pierced the secret," he said.

In Washington it was no secret just how violent had become the opposition from the Pentagon and its hawkish, arms-supply allies toward Diana's meddling in their affairs. At this point, I was told by my international intelligence source, the ruthless element of the American arms interests felt ready to order the disposal of the troublesome princess. Diana had incensed American and international military and industrial forces with her land mines campaign sufficiently for them to want to be rid of her.

President Bill Clinton had created a new wave of outrage among domestic opponents, including the Pentagon, just twelve days earlier on August 18, by publicly confirming he would vote in favor of a land mines ban on September 19. This had launched a frenzied lobbying of the president from all angles.

Now, it was believed, the princess was considering championing the cause of Gulf War Syndrome victims, a hugely politically sensitive issue and one which the Establishment oligarchs—and their

American counterparts—could not countenance. There was also talk of her being nominated for a Nobel Peace Prize which could only have inflated her potency against the arms manufacturers and dealers and their military customers.

For some, simply protecting the royal family from further scandal and ensuring Prince Charles a relatively smooth path to fulfilling his destiny, including his determination to marry Camilla, was reason enough to be rid of her. Other factors would have merely added to the attraction of the solution and made it impossible to turn it down, explained one former intelligence agent.

Time was rapidly running out for the Americans, whose deadline for action was September 19 before Clinton signed that land mines ban. Intelligence officers and agents from the CIA and MI6 had kept Princess Diana under twenty-four-hour-a-day surveillance for weeks, awaiting, said the ex-intelligence man, a favorable opportunity to strike. The essential criteria still, even at this late stage, was that the assassination must appear to be an accident. Time was also running out for those in England who believed she was pregnant: soon the signs would become unmistakable. If the opportunity could be created, then Paris would be the location where their problems would, hopefully, be resolved.

Her visit to Paris with Dodi was the first feasible occasion to make the attempt. The plan would not be perfect, certainly not foolproof, and would rely, to a large extent, on part-time agents. But if the target could be placed in a car, traveling at high speed and preferably at night, on a route devised—and thus known in advance—by them, there was an excellent chance of success. MI6 was extremely proficient at arranging last-minute operations like this, says Richard Tomlinson. In almost identical circumstances, where opportunities to stage a fatal accident would be few, MI6 had already devised an assassination plan, he said.

"The intended victim was President Slobodan Milosevic of Serbia in 1992, and it was proposed he should be killed in a staged crash as his car passed into a motorway tunnel on his way to Geneva. A blinding strobe light would be used. I read the dossier at the time, while I was based in the Balkans. Diana's killing would occur in the precise circumstances spelled out in the MI6 officer's proposal I had been shown back then."

On the actual morning that Diana was murdered, the *Sunday Mirror* published a major story on the couple. It read, in part:

At Balmoral next week the Queen will preside over a meeting of The Way Ahead Group where the Windsors sit down with their senior advisers and discuss policy matters.

MI6 has prepared a special report on the Egyptian Fayeds which will be presented to the meeting.

Prince Philip has let rip several times recently about the Fayeds—at a dinner party, during a country shoot and while on a visit to close friends in Germany. He's been banging on about his contempt for Dodi and how he is undesirable as a future stepfather to William and Harry. Diana has been told in no uncertain terms about the consequences should she continue the relationship with the Fayed boy . . . now the royal family may have decided it is time to settle up.

Without the total cooperation of the American, French and British governments, the French judiciary, police and intelligence forces, and access to the files of the CIA and MI6, it will never be possible to identify positively, by name, the actual people who ordered Princess Diana's murder, or give the precise circumstances of her death. To do so would be to drift into the realm of fantasy. But I believe it is safe to conclude that by August 31, 1997, one would have needed to be absolutely, or deliberately, blind not to have recognized the overwhelming desire by her enemies, on both sides of the Atlantic, to be rid of her. To pretend otherwise is simply to ignore the evidence.

The deeply flawed, eighteen-month, secret judicial investigation rejected any suggestion of foul play, or the possibility of an organized assassination. The case is irrevocably closed, say the French authorities, even though its controversial conclusion, which blamed the driver alone for the crash, has become hopelessly discredited and tarnished.

Eighty-five percent of the British public are convinced that their verdict was wrong.

TEN

The Fayed nerve center in Paris, the elegant
and world renowned Ritz Hotel, had sent two vehicles to collect Dodi and his party from Le Bourget
airport. One was a luxury, black Mercedes 600 limousine with tinted windows, driven by Philippe
Dourneau, who was under permanent contract as
Dodi's chauffeur. The other, Dodi's personal black
Range Rover, was driven by Henri Paul, the acting
head of security at the Ritz Hotel. Diana had met
the balding, bespectacled security chief on her
previous trip to the hotel with Dodi, and she and
her lover stood chatting with him for several minutes before boarding the Mercedes.

Strictly speaking, Henri Paul should not have
been there. He had scheduled himself off the rota
for the weekend and had planned a trip to the
country. One of his oldest friends, Dominique
Melo, a psychiatrist at the University of Rennes,
said, "As soon as he learned Dodi and Diana were

coming to Paris from Sardinia he canceled a short break that he had fixed in Lorient to see his parents."

Trevor Rees-Jones, as bodyguard, was detailed to travel with Dodi and Diana in the front passenger seat of the Mercedes. It was noted by Philippe that Diana and Dodi did not fasten their seat belts in the back. When accompanied by her Royal Protection Squad officer, Diana had always been made to fasten her seat belt as part of a rigid overall safety routine, but a year later she had fallen out of the habit of buckling up her belt when traveling in the back seat—and the Al Fayed security men did not insist, partly, it must be said, because Dodi did not favor using a rear belt and would probably have countermanded their instructions.

Philippe was a superb driver and within minutes had shaken off the paparazzi swarm as he skillfully maneuvered the big Mercedes around the *périphérique*, the circular Paris motorway, to the Bois de Boulogne exit ramp to the west of central Paris. Their first stop, twenty-five minutes' drive from the airport, was the Villa Windsor. Hand in hand, the couple toured the house where the Duke of Windsor had lived in exile with his American bride, Wallis Simpson. Twenty years earlier Mohamed Al Fayed had acquired a lease on the property from the French government, and had spent a fortune refurbishing it. Dodi tried to persuade Princess Diana that this was one of the houses in which they should make their home. But Diana was not overly impressed. She thought it was too gloomy.

Meanwhile, as the lovers made their brief tour of the house—admiring the five acres of gardens from the upper windows—Henri Paul had taken René, the butler, two female members of the *Jonikal* crew and the luggage to Dodi's Paris apartment, and driven with the second bodyguard, Alexander "Kez" Wingfield, to join the others at Villa Windsor.

Just twenty-eight minutes after their arrival, according to the CCTV cameras at the villa, Diana and Dodi climbed back into their car for the short journey to the Ritz Hotel in the Place Vendôme. Henri Paul followed behind in convoy in the Range Rover. A number of paparazzi were there to take pictures, clearly having received a further tip-off about the party's movements. When they arrived at the luxurious hotel entrance, the paparazzi were already waiting in some force, but the transfer from car to foyer was accomplished smoothly under the supervision of the acting hotel manager Claude Roulet. Shortly after 4:30 P.M. they were once more safely installed inside the Imperial Suite.

One of Diana's first tasks was to telephone confidant and friend, journalist Richard Kay, then royal correspondent and now diarist of the *Daily Mail*. In his report of that telephone call, Kay was able to reveal that the princess had told him, "I have decided to radically change my life." She would complete her obligations to her charities and to the anti-land mines campaign and would then, around November, completely withdraw from public life. He was also able to confide in readers that "Diana was as happy as I have ever known her. For the first time in years all was well with her world." Richard Kay felt able to say that Diana was in love with Dodi and that she believed him to be in love with her, and that he also believed in her.

The journalist did not speculate on why Diana intended to change her lifestyle, but others, who had for two weeks heard much discussion about Diana's bulging figure and rumors that she was pregnant, believed this outpouring to Richard Kay was yet another hint that the princess was expecting a baby.

After making her call to London, Diana went down to the hairdressing salon by the Ritz swimming pool to have a wash and blow-dry before dinner, and Dodi went to collect the ring from Repossi's jewelery boutique. It was no more than a hundred yards' walk across the Place Vendôme to the boutique, but Dodi chose to drive there in the Mercedes, taking Trevor Rees-Jones with him. Kez Wingfield and Claude Roulet followed on foot and the three men waited outside while Dodi went in to collect the £130,000 emerald-and-diamond ring.

By seven o' clock they were both ready to leave the Imperial Suite and transfer to Dodi's apartment where they would change for dinner and where butler René had chilled wine and caviar waiting. They had already reserved a table at Diana's favorite Parisian restaurant, Chez Benoit on the edge of Les Halles. People around them couldn't help smiling as they watched Dodi choreograph an evening which was obviously planned as a build-up to a formal marriage proposal.

Philippe Dourneau would continue as their driver in the Mercedes 600, but for this journey they would be without the bodyguards. Lack of professionalism led to Trevor and Kez breaking one of

the golden rules of personal protection. To "give
the couple some time to themselves" the two bodyguards elected to travel in a separate follow-up vehicle, the Range Rover, which was being driven
that evening by Jean-Francis Musa, the owner of
the Etoile Limousines company which rented cars
to the Ritz.

Had the two vehicles become separated, the results could have been disastrous. As it was, their
journey to the rue Arsène Houssaye, near the
junction of the Champs Elysées and the Arc de
Triomphe, was smooth and uneventful, but on
their arrival outside the apartment, where the bulk
of the paparazzi had been congregating, it was
utter bedlam. Trevor and Kez believed, not for the
first time that summer, that the photographers
must have been tipped off in advance about the
party's movements. Led by Romuald Rat, a bulky,
menacing six-footer who was screaming at the
bodyguards, they swarmed aggressively around the
couple, shouting abuse at Dodi and Diana and
thrusting camera lenses right into their faces.

Even Diana, with years of experience with photographers, was frightened by the savagery of this
frenzy, each paparazzo being aware of the vast
sums of money now on offer for the right pictures
and allowing greed to take over from whatever
professionalism they might still have retained. For
Diana, celebrity had long coexisted with the mantle of royalty, but since her divorce, the media's
natural reluctance to encroach too far into royal
space had, like the royal mantle itself, slipped
rapidly away. Now only the celebrity remained
and, no longer protected by that royal aura which

she had once taken for granted, she had become vulnerable. It was a frightening new development and not one with which she could easily come to terms.

When they finally reached his luxurious apartment, Dodi was white with anger and frustration—and perhaps a hint of humiliation that the Al Fayed security was not proving as effective as he had boasted it would be. Shaken, but otherwise undamaged, they tucked in to caviar and an excellent chilled white wine, and were soon smiling again as the sheer happiness of their relationship won through.

It was here that their luggage had been brought from the airport that afternoon, and their things had already been unpacked and pressed. Soon it was time for them to change for dinner. Diana chose calf-hugging, white Versace jeans with high-heeled Versace black slingbacks and a sleeveless black top under a black Versace blazer. With this she wore a pearl necklace given to her by Dodi, gold earrings and a Jaeger Le Coultre watch.

Dodi had picked out Calvin Klein blue jeans over brown cowboy boots, a gray Daniel Hechter leather shirt, worn outside his jeans and with which he was unable to wear Diana's latest gift of cufflinks that had belonged to her father, and a casual brown, soft suede jacket. His jewelry included a Cartier watch and a metal identity disc, engraved with "Fayed. Blood Group B Positive." He also took with him cigars, a cigar cutter and his mobile phone, none of which was found in the Mercedes after the crash. Was some clue contained within his mobile phone's memory of a call he made, that necessitated his phone being seized by the killers? Or were these personal items simply plundered by the rescue workers?

Just after 9:30 P.M. they again ran the gauntlet of jostling paparazzi, whose onslaught was only slightly less hostile, and settled into the limousine. Trevor and Kez again elected to follow in the Range Rover. This time their astonishingly unprofessional decision for one of them not to travel with Diana came very close to endangering their charges.

Dodi believed that with the number of photographers currently on the streets, a quiet dinner in Chez Benoit was out of the question, and he canceled their reservation on his mobile phone. His next call was to Trevor Rees-Jones, in the backup Range Rover, to advise him that they were returning directly to the Ritz Hotel. Trevor knew that stand-in hotel boss Claude Roulet was outside the Chez Benoit, where he had planned to orchestrate their arrival and dinner, and that there was no one else left at the hotel to respond to such a last-minute call for extra security. They were already turning into the Place Vendôme where they could see a crowd of photographers and tourists jostling one another for vantage points outside the Ritz entrance, which already numbered over a hundred. The Ritz security cameras had noted that several of these had been there all day, observing from the edges of the crowd, but not falling into the category of tourists or photographers. Ex-Scotland Yard de~~tective chief superintendent~~ John McNamara, ~~who~~ headed the Ritz–Fayed investigation into the crash, later identified them as British and foreign intelligence agents.

As the mini-convoy pulled up, and the two body-guards rushed forward to the limousine, the crowd closed in from all sides, flashbulbs popping. But when Trevor opened the limousine door, Dodi did not respond. He just sat there, apparently frozen. No one moved for several seconds, and any advantage they may have had of surprise was lost.

A bodyguard inside the Mercedes could have motivated his passengers to move the moment the car stopped.

When the princess, who obviously saw the situation deteriorating, did emerge, she was almost immediately engulfed. Looking terrified, she jumped over people's legs and ran, swaying from side to side, for the Ritz front door. With luck, and sheer athletic wizardry, she made it inside and collapsed on a chair in the foyer.

Dodi, helped by Kez and Trevor, was moments behind, and blazing mad. As Trevor threw an intruding photographer back into the street the Fayed heir exploded, "How the fuck did this fiasco happen?"

Kez Wingfield, himself angry, and close, he said later, to hitting his boss, snarled back, "You never told us where we were going in time. If you had, we'd have been able to phone ahead and get it sorted out."

Dodi had the sense to back off and turned his full attention to Diana. He guided her to the hotel's prestigious L'Espadon restaurant, but found the princess still far too agitated to cope with the staring gaze of dozens of wealthy, but still gawking, diners. In tears, she asked to be taken up to the Imperial Suite to eat in private.

It was still their intention to return to Dodi's flat

when things quieted down. But instead of quieting down they heated up. Outside the Ritz there was a sort of madness swirling among the paparazzi. Because of the rumors now being circulated in London that Diana was pregnant, they had come from all over Europe—each hoping for another million-pound picture. The princess had been photographed in a swimsuit which revealed a slight bulge in her tummy. She had told a friend that the bump was fat and that she planned on having it removed by liposuction. But the newspapers—and the paparazzi—remained unconvinced.

Still scattered among the crowd, too, and picked up later by examination of closed-circuit television tapes, were the same British, French and American security service agents.

It was also later established that the personal secretary to the head of Britain's MI6 had spent the weekend in Paris. No explanation has ever been offered for why the agents were mingling with the crowd outside the hotel, but Richard Tomlinson says an unusually high number of his former colleagues were in town that night. He said they included two senior officers who were there on an "undeclared" basis. "I believe either, or both of them would have detailed knowledge of events affecting Princess Diana that night," he said.

A few minutes after 10 P.M., Henri Paul arrived back in the hotel. He had been called in, at Dodi's bidding, by his night security manager, François Fendel. "Dodi is on top of the world, but he would appreciate you coming in," Fendel told his boss. "It would help to calm things down."

Thus, the man who had canceled his weekend off to play a central part in the lovers' Paris visit was back in a position to influence the most crucial event of the evening. Henri Paul's first move was to join Kez and Trevor, who were planning to eat in the restaurant bar. They chatted and Henri Paul had two drinks before going off to do his rounds. On his return, security inside the hotel had automatically passed from the bodyguards to him. Trevor and Kez remember that he in no way seemed on edge, was definitely not drunk, and that there was nothing in his behavior that caused them any alarm. From the Ritz records that night, it was shown that Henri Paul had drunk just two pastis—a spirits-strength drink taken with five parts water to one of pastis. They were the only drinks he consumed during his two hours and ten minutes in the hotel.

It has never been established where he went, or what he was doing, during the three hours between leaving the Ritz at 7 P.M. and receiving the call from Fendel at 10 P.M. It is perfectly possible, as no one can positively remember seeing him in his usual haunts during that period, that he was at home. He had told Dodi, before leaving at 7 P.M., that he would be available to give any assistance for the rest of the night if he should be needed. It is highly unlikely that he would have risked alienating his boss by turning up drunk if he were recalled. Losing his job would cost him £35,000 a year from the international intelligence market, in addition to his £20,000 salary.

"And as an agent of MI6 he probably had an even better reason to remain sober," said Richard Tomlinson. During the day Henri Paul had acquired £2,000 in cash which he was carrying in his pocket and which the police would discover was still on him after the crash. According to American investigative journalist Gerald Posner, Henri Paul was indeed involved in his clandestine work. He quotes an American law-enforcement official and an American intelligence officer who told him Paul spent the hours before he returned to the hotel with an agent from the DGSE (*Direction Général de la Sécurité Extérieure*—the French equivalent of the CIA). The sum of £8,000 had been paid into several of Paul's bank accounts in the past few weeks— since Diana and Dodi had become close. This was only a part of the £140,000-plus which he had ac- crued in seven bank accounts in the past few years— earnings from his MI6 and other intelligence-agency work.

Was the latest cash payment, as Tomlinson sus- pects, to cover Henri Paul's efforts yet to come during that weekend? Was his main task to influ- ence the route they would follow if they left the hotel again that night? To persuade Dodi he must go back to the apartment?

Said his close friend and neighbor Claude Garric, "I knew all along that Henri did work for intelli- gence agencies. He was in touch with the British secret service and the Israelis and others. The hotel had important clients from all over the world. He did have alcoholic drinks at home, but his favorite drink was Coca-Cola Light and he had 240 bottles of this when the police went to his home the next day. He almost invariably drank Coca-Cola at home. I had the key and let them in. They were only in- terested in listing the few alcoholic drinks that were there. They didn't bother writing down the names or the quantities of soft drinks. Their search was focused on alcohol. They even wrote down the names of alcoholic drinks they claimed they had found, which were not there. They found no medication in the apartment of any description."

Three friends who had regular weekly dinners with Henri Paul did not know him as a big drinker. At Chez Armand, one of the favorite haunts of the four friends, the manager said Paul usually had a pastis and a couple of glasses of wine with his meal. "He never drank much."

The manager of Le Grand Colbert where they also ate regularly said, "Nobody ever got drunk. Henri Paul was not a heavy drinker."

Just three days before the crash he had undergone his annual medical as a private pilot. He had passed all the tests, including urine, reflexes, hand–eye coordination and mental health. He had never had a health or drink problem in the twenty-five years since he had been attracted to a flying club near his home town of Lorient when he was still only fifteen. He obtained his private pilot's license when he was sixteen.

Kez Wingfield and Trevor Rees-Jones saw him on several occasions in the two hours after he returned to the hotel, and at no stage did he act as though he had been drinking. CCTV footage shows him to have been behaving impeccably. At one stage he is seen squatting down to tie a shoelace. He switches his weight from one foot to the other, and then rises gracefully and effortlessly, an extremely unlikely event had he had the amount of drink, drugs and carbon monoxide in his bloodstream which the police later claimed was the case. He would have been more likely to have toppled on his side, say medical experts.

Henri Paul had worked in the Ritz security ser-

vice since it was first established eleven years earlier, and was considered a model employee. His
loyalty and professionalism were highly rated by
the Fayeds, and he was a particular favorite of
Dodi's.

Shortly before 10:30 P.M., Dodi had spoken to
the hotel night manager, Thierry Rocher, and told
him that their intention was to return to the apartment. He asked Rocher to tell Henri Paul to contact him in the suite for a conference and
instructions.

Dodi had already, say his family, formally proposed to Diana, and in a telephone call to his father the princess is said to have confirmed they
were to marry, and that she had finally found, in
Dodi, the man who would make her happy. The
Sunday People later arranged a taped interview with
Mohamed Al Fayed, in which he reiterated what
he claimed Diana had told him. They had the
recording tested by the finest forensic criminolo-
gist in America, Dr. Steven Laub, using the latest
lie-detecting equipment. After six hours of tests
Dr. Laub reported, "I am convinced he is telling
the truth."

It would certainly explain why Dodi and Diana
were so keen to return to the familiar intimacy of
his apartment rather than consummate their engagement in the impersonal surroundings of the
Imperial Suite—however luxurious and expensive
it might be. An hour later Dodi told Thierry
Rocher that they would be leaving from the back
entrance in the rue Cambon. He was satisfied that
Henri Paul could take care of himself and the
princess and drive them to his apartment. Dodi
told Rocher to organize an extra car, to be taken

to the rear entrance after midnight. The two vehicles used earlier would remain outside the front entrance to act as decoys when the moment came for departure.

It has to be assumed that Henri Paul had used some very persuasive arguments in order to convince Dodi to scrap all the rules his father had drummed into him and the family for twenty years or more. In a single conversation he had arranged, with Dodi, to change all of the hotel's, and Al Fayed's, long-standing security regulations. These were actually written down in a manual and known to the bodyguards by heart. One instruction, covering the movement of VIPs, stated that the personal bodyguard and up to seven other bodyguards must operate within the immediate area of the VIP, and be directly responsible for the VIP's safety at all times. Whenever Al Fayed moved, he used an armored limousine, a backup car and eight bodyguards. Dodi was now proposing to take the world's most famous woman across Paris in a single car with no bodyguard in attendance, on the simple assurance of his friend and acting security chief.

At 11:30 P.M., Henri Paul went to the Imperial Suite, where Kez and Trevor were seated outside waiting for instructions, and told the stunned bodyguards that they would not be traveling with Dodi and the princess. He, Henri Paul, would be responsible for driving them and for their safety. No second backup vehicle or bodyguard would be needed. "We will be leaving in half an hour," he told them. "And you will be with the decoy vehicles."

Was this Henri Paul, Ritz Hotel employee, talking; or was it Henri Paul, paid lackey of MI6, setting Dodi and Diana up for a surprise? And was he, in turn, being set up by MI6 and the CIA for a surprise of a very different kind?

Trevor's anger was instantaneous. "No fucking way is he leaving without a bodyguard—no way in a million years it's going to be without me. I'll be coming with you if we go with this," he told Henri Paul.

When Kez added that they would have to report the plans to London, Henri Paul told him, "It has already been OK'd by Mohamed Al Fayed." It was a difficult call to make for the two bodyguards. They had no easy way of checking Paul's statement without causing offense—and possibly being sacked. But this plan went against all their training. It was a situation unprecedented in their combined experience as bodyguards and close-protection specialists.

Moments later, almost as though on cue, Dodi emerged from the suite and confirmed Henri Paul's instructions. Only one car would leave from the back with Henri driving. Trevor remembers being forceful. "You aren't leaving without security," he told Dodi. "I'll be coming." When Dodi refused to consider an alternative plan, Trevor dug in his heels. "There's absolutely no way you're going without security," he told his boss.

"OK. One of you can come in the car, in the front," Dodi finally relented. But on the subject of a backup car he refused to budge, and returned to the Imperial Suite, leaving the bodyguards with a situation that, however much they hated it, they had to get on and work with.

Trevor called in Philippe and Musa, who were on standby in the Etoile Limousines offices opposite the Ritz, and told them to organize an extra car. As he was briefing them, Claude Roulet, who had returned unexpectedly to the hotel, joined in. He had clearly already talked to Dodi or Henri Paul and told Musa to lay on another car immediately. It would be driven by Henri Paul. Musa knew that Henri Paul was not officially licensed to drive the replacement limousine which he planned to use, but in the tension of the moment no one seemed prepared to make a big thing out of this. Henri Paul was qualified on his ordinary license to drive a Mercedes S280—the proposed replacement car. But in France the police insist on a special license to drive a large limousine for hire. If Henri Paul had convinced Dodi he could get them home that night, then Claude Roulet was not about to split hairs about a special license being needed, or about backup security. He simply wanted his boss's son to be happy.

Meanwhile in the Imperial Suite Kez was trying one last appeal with Dodi. "Two cars are best," he said.

But Dodi silenced him. "It's been OK'd by my father." The matter was closed.

Al Fayed would later deny he knew anything, that night, about the plan for Henri Paul to drive to his son's apartment. When Dodi had telephoned saying he would feel safer with Diana at his apartment, Al Fayed had told him that if he had any doubts at all then he should stay in the Imperial Suite which provided the best luxury and security that money could buy. "Paul convinced my son that he should go to the apartment. That all their things were there," said Mohamed Al Fayed later. "He said they should leave from the back entrance and he would get them home. He changed Dodi's mind and persuaded him to go along with him. That it was safe."

After his earlier conversation with the bodyguards, Henri Paul appeared at the front entrance to the hotel on several occasions, calling to the paparazzi that Diana would be leaving soon. He seemed to be trying to convince them that she would be leaving by that entrance. But some suspicious photographers had already decided to go around to the rue Cambon entrance and wait there. They would remain in constant telephone communication with their fellow hunters at the front.

Shortly after midnight, Frederic Lucard, who worked as a chauffeur at Etoile Limousines, was told to drive a Mercedes S280—registration number 688 LTV 75—to the rue Cambon entrance. It was a standard limousine with neither bulletproof armor nor darkened windows.

At 12:14 A.M., Dodi and the princess left the Imperial Suite, laughing and looking very relaxed and happy. A few glasses of wine had obviously worked their magic and the princess's tears of two hours earlier were just a distant memory. They went straight down one flight of stairs, which led them to the back entrance, and waited in a narrow service corridor. A smiling Henri Paul chatted to them while Trevor kept watch for the limousine. As he looked out, he remembers spotting a small hatchback—a three-door car that was either white or light in color, with a trunk that opened at the back, a car which could easily have been a Fiat Uno—and perhaps a scooter or motorcycle with two or three journalists.

At 12:19 A.M., as the Mercedes arrived, the security cameras captured Dodi sliding a hand gently to the small of Diana's back.

The changeover went smoothly. Frederic Lucard gave the keys to Henri Paul and, as the tubby security chief slid confidently behind the wheel, Trevor Rees-Jones shepherded his charges, Diana with her eyes lowered as flashbulbs lanced the darkness around them, into the back. Then he took his place in front.

Trevor alerted Kez, in the Mercedes in front of the hotel, that they were about to move. Two minutes later the original Mercedes and the Range Rover sprinted away. The decoy was running but the birds had already flown. Most of the paparazzi were either already in, or on their way to the rue Cambon where, at 12:20 A.M., Henri Paul had pulled away from the Ritz back entrance at speed and with flashbulbs still popping.

One of the last things Trevor remembers is the white or light-colored car following them—that and the fact that Henri Paul, at that moment, appeared absolutely normal and sober and completely in control. Kez Wingfield is also adamant that Henri Paul was totally sober at all times when he saw him in the hotel that night. Both men swear that had there been the slightest hint or indication that Henri Paul was other than completely sober, they would have removed him from the plan rather than risk the safety of their charges. They would never knowingly have allowed a drunk man to drive, they said. They had been extremely close to Henri Paul on several occasions, and neither of them had noticed any whiff of alcohol on his breath. Night security manager

François Tendil, hotel night manager Thierry Rochet and Claude Roulet, the Ritz's number two, also swear that Henri Paul conducted himself perfectly normally and gave no sign, either by movement or voice, of having been drinking.

ELEVEN

As the black Mercedes S280 carrying Diana, Princess of Wales and Dodi Fayed was driven down the one-way rue Cambon, photographers were still snapping pictures of them through the plain-glass windows. Some were already mounting their motorcycles, preparing to give chase, but the couple would have believed at that point that they had only a little more than five minutes of exposure left before arriving at Dodi's apartment, less than a mile-and-a-half away.

As Henri Paul steered the big car right into the rue de Rivoli, some of the paparazzi, who had been waiting at the front entrance of the Ritz in the Place Vendôme, were streaming out of the rue de Castiglione into the same major thoroughfare, but 150 yards to their rear. At this moment, no one was doing anything stupid. All it required was for Henri Paul to drive at a reasonable speed straight up the Champs Elysées. The worst that could happen, if they were forced to stop at traffic lights, was that the paparazzi may get a few more sideways shots of the lovers. There could be no life-threatening incidents on this, the widest, straightest and best-policed avenue in the French capital.

Except, Richard Tomlinson believes, that one of the central characters involved, Henri Paul, was marching to the beat of a different drum to the others being conveyed in the Mercedes that night—and would not be taking the expected route. The acting security chief of the Ritz had his own agenda, and what happened next, it is believed, was exactly what had all along been intended. One thing is utterly certain: the final outcome was not the finale that had been promised to Henri Paul. He too was to prove a gullible victim of Diana's killers.

If one accepts the premise that the wad of cash in Paul's pocket, and the recent huge payments into his secret bank accounts, were to pay for his cooperation in an arranged incident, then what happened next was all part of the plan dictated by his intelligence paymasters. At the traffic lights outside the Crillon Hotel he turned the car left into the Place de la Concorde. But then, instead of going almost immediately right into the Champs Elysées and taking the shortest, safest and most direct route to Dodi's apartment, he continued south along the west side of the square, past the Paris twin of Cleopatra's needle in London, almost as far as the river Seine. There he cut the traffic lights on red, and swung the Mercedes right onto the fast-track dual freeway Cours la Reine. This put him on a heading parallel to the river, and at an angle fifty degrees at variance with his intended destination. And he was speeding up.

Hervé Stephan, the judge in charge of the crash investigation never bothered to investigate why Henri Paul had taken this very indirect route to Dodi's apartment.

Almost immediately after joining the Cours la Reine they entered the first of a series of tunnels which are designed to keep traffic on this central city freeway moving smoothly. By the end of this 300-yard tunnel, which stretched between the two bridges, Pont des Invalides and Pont Alexandre III, Henri Paul had already put a considerable distance between himself and the paparazzi, who were showing no particular eagerness to catch up. There would be few opportunities to take a decent picture en route. Unlike the Champs Elysées, this route was not well lit, and the backcloth of darkness and the unlighted interior of the car would cause too many reflections off the windows to capture a decent shot of the occupants. There would be plenty of time and opportunity to take their pictures, they rationalized, when they reached journey's end. Most of those who were later interviewed said they envisaged another chaotic crowd outside Dodi's apartment. Many of the pack had already assumed where their destination would be and had given up the chase. These had peeled off at the Champs Elysées to go directly to the rue Arsène Houssaye.

At least one other vehicle, however, was heading in the same direction as the Mercedes, and on the same road—a white Fiat Uno, possibly the same hatchback spotted by Trevor Rees-Jones in the rue Cambon and earlier in the Place Vendôme, and almost certainly driven by a well-known personality among the paparazzi, James Andanson, another sometime employee of MI6. A millionaire with a murky past, he would later lie to the French police about having been in Paris that night. As I will explain more fully later, Andanson was already under investigation by the French equivalent of Special Branch, who were reinvestigating the alleged suicide of former prime minister Pierre Bérégovoy.

Curiously, the Fiat was in front of the Mercedes. Richard Tomlinson believed that Andanson had no need to follow Henri Paul, because he knew precisely which route they were both taking.

As he passed the last turnoff, on the Cours Albert Ier, 350 yards before the Alma tunnel, Henri Paul was driving at a steady 64 miles per hour (102 kilometers per hour), though it would take a further six years to discover this known statistic from a speed-camera printout and photograph, the existence of which police consistently denied. He might have turned off there, up the slip road leading to the Avenue George V which led almost straight to Dodi's apartment, still nearly a mile away.

They had already traveled more than a mile, and each extra yard now covered would take them farther away from their destination.

A witness would tell later that a motorcyclist had stopped in the middle of the exit ramp on the Cours Albert Ier, effectively blocking it to traffic. But Henri Paul nevertheless apparently made no attempt to take this slip-road exit, and it was assumed it was not his intention to do so.

Another explanation is that he had been told to drive through the Alma tunnel by undercover agents who were paying him.

Just yards from the entrance to the Alma tunnel, the Mercedes had pulled into the left-hand lane of the outside freeway. Henri Paul was obliged to do this in order to pass the Fiat Uno, still ahead of them and in the right-hand lane. It had been crawling along shortly before the tunnel entrance, and had now begun to pick up speed. Police have refused to say whether it was also photographed by the speed camera which logged the Mercedes.

Just before they arrived in the tunnel, a motorcycle with a pillion passenger had passed them and taken a lead position in front of the two cars. The motorcyclist and his passenger were never identified, and therefore it remains unknown if they were photographers. Certainly at this moment the nearest identifiable paparazzi were still traveling in a swarm at least half a mile behind.

As the Mercedes reached the tunnel and was about to cross the notorious hump at its entrance, two things occurred almost simultaneously: first a speed camera, set in the tunnel roof, took a photograph of the Mercedes, the flash showing Henri Paul to be looking normal, Trevor Rees-Jones slightly apprehensive and the couple in the back laughing; and second, the Fiat Uno, still gaining speed, eased left into the path of the Mercedes. It is beyond coincidence that this particular car and driver, who had dawdled in the approaches to the tunnel so obviously awaiting the arrival of the Mercedes, should speed up and deliberately swerve into its path, precisely on the threshold of the most notorious black spot on the river freeway. It was at this precise point the driver could be guaranteed to do the most damage, and then be in a position to speed away after the crash without stopping to offer assistance.

Henri Paul was forced to swerve violently to the left in order to avoid a major collision with the smaller car, but he wasn't quite fast enough to miss it completely. He clipped the left-hand side of the rear bumper and the red taillight of the Fiat with his right wing mirror, wing and front door as the cars swept down into the dip in the road which follows the hump. This may have been the moment when an alarmed Trevor Rees-Jones snatched his seat belt across his chest. He did not succeed in buckling up. What he says he does remember now is that on three separate occasions he had told the couple in the back to fasten their seat belts, and that they had failed to comply.

The Mercedes was now angled toward the center of the dual freeway, which at this point began to bend quite sharply to the left. Henri Paul's left flick of the wheel to avoid the smaller car might in itself have been slightly hazardous, but need not, in normal circumstances, have proved fatal.

But these were far from normal circumstances.

According to one witness, at the same moment that Henri Paul turned the Mercedes left in an attempt to avoid collision with the Fiat Uno—almost at the precise instant, in fact, when the two cars touched, the pillion passenger on the motorcycle in front turned around and suddenly directed the full glare of an immensely powerful hand-held searchlight at the limousine's windshield. A second witness, following in a car behind, spoke of seeing a bright flash, which she thought was from a camera, from beyond the Mercedes, a split second before the crash.

Lights such as these are used as weapons by the SAS in surprise raids. They blind and mentally disorient the enemy for up to a full minute. A senior SAS officer told me, "The effect on a driver, at night particularly, is catastrophic. He is totally blinded and mentally stunned. He would be incapable of steering a car. Indeed any bright light directed suddenly in the driver's eyes at that moment, when he had been forced to swerve left, would have had lethal consequences." Suddenly blind and utterly disoriented in the midst of a tricky steering maneuver, at sixty-four miles per hour and running so close to the central concrete pillars, he stood very little chance.

There are no crash barriers in the Alma tunnel and no safety walls to scrape along. Said Richard Tomlinson, "A tunnel is a perfect place for an assassination." It has fewer witnesses, and the Paris tunnel is ideal because there are no crash railings along the central pillars which separate the two freeways. It is deadly.

In his perilous predicament, Henri Paul may have pushed the automatic gear lever into neutral, frantically searching for a lower gear to slow the car without fierce braking; this could account for the racing engine noise that some witnesses describe. But, as with every other aspect of the crash, the police have absolutely refused to say if the car was in gear or in neutral. Nor, they say, will they ever do so.

In the split second that was all Henri Paul had

to act, he did not skid and he did not brake. There were tire marks on the road, but road-accident experts say they were not caused by Diana's car.

Then the Mercedes S280, still traveling at sixty-four miles per hour, ran headlong into the thirteenth concrete pillar in the central dividing reservation. The airbags all functioned on impact, but as none of the passengers was restrained by seat belts they gave minimal protection.

Dodi Fayed and Henri Paul died almost instantly. Trevor Rees-Jones was knocked unconscious and had, literally, the whole of the front of his face ripped away.

Diana received a massive, and eventually fatal, internal injury when her body was hurled violently by the car's momentum against the seat in front. She wasn't trapped, as even though the front had been almost totally crushed on impact, the rear of the car was relatively undamaged. Diana was lodged in the well between the back seat and the passenger seat in front.

Smoke, steam and water were spurting from the shattered engine, and the blast of the horn eerily reverberated along the tunnel and into the night in the Place de l'Alma above.

The Fiat Uno and the motorcycle were already exiting the tunnel at the far end.

"Everything had happened," said Richard Tomlinson, "exactly as specified in the MI6 plan to kill Slobodan Milosevic."

Explained ex-MI5 officer David Shayler, "Vehicle 'accidents' are used as a way of assassination precisely because they are such a common cause of death. It is easy for the authorities to claim that anyone crying foul play is simply a 'conspiracy theorist.' "

Unless Trevor Rees-Jones recovers his memory, or decides to speak out, no one will ever know, for certain, the exact details of the murder of Princess Diana, Dodi Fayed and Henri Paul, but the evidence now available six years after the crash indicates that the description I have given is accurate in all its essential details. One of the only other men who might have provided the full story, James Andanson, who would later boast to friends that he witnessed the death of Diana, was himself found dead in extremely suspicious circumstances in May 2000.

This was an opportunist killing. Had her assassins not succeeded in this murder attempt, and had the princess survived the crash, there would have been further opportunities to finish the job. The senior SAS officer told me, "Something could have been arranged in the time between the crash and her being transferred to hospital. Or there could easily have occurred a 'regrettable medical accident' in the hospital, leading to her death. Such things have happened before. And had the attempt had to be aborted that night, another opportunity would no doubt have presented itself before too long. If a professional assassination squad wanted her dead, then sooner or later they would have succeeded. The odds would not have been on her side."

I have driven through the Alma tunnel myself, in a similar-sized car, and in excess of sixty-five miles per hour. I entered the tunnel in the left lane and swerved the car suddenly left, as Henri

Paul did, just before the crash pillar. I was able to correct the steering, despite the dip, without difficulty.

I would also stress that I am not a professional driver.

The Mercedes was doing just sixty-four miles per hour, as the French police well know, despite their trying to perpetuate the myth that it was traveling much faster. When Scotland Yard senior detectives visited the tunnel in April 2004, it was stated that an unnamed racing driver had refused to go through the tunnel at seventy-five miles per hour, saying, reportedly, that it was much too risky. There are dips and turns on the Monaco Grand Prix circuit which are much more dangerous and taken at much higher speeds. In my opinion this was just another public-relations stunt to support the Paris police's deliberately distorted version of events.

I am convinced that, had it not been for the intervention of the Fiat Uno and the bright light being directed through the windshield and dazzling Henri Paul, he would almost certainly not have crashed the car that night.

One other extremely disturbing fact which emerged during my investigation is the existence, in the official judicial file, of a photograph—not the one taken by the Alma tunnel speed camera—but one that is taken from the same level as the Mercedes, and directly from the front, showing all four of its occupants.

It must have been taken either from the Fiat Uno, which I will later show was driven by a French paparazzo, working for British intelligence—a man who boasted to friends of having been there "at the death," or from the motorcycle from which the flash was fired.

According to a Paris lawyer with access to the official files, it was taken inside the Alma Tunnel, and can only have been snatched a second or two before the crash. That certainly makes it the last photograph taken of Princess Diana, Dodi Fayed and Henri Paul alive.

TWELVE

One hour after the crash that killed Diana, senior French police, judicial and political figures who were already conferring at the spot—and being counseled from the shadows by telephone—came up with a simple answer to the carnage in the Alma tunnel, and one that would be popularly acceptable to the public: the wretched paparazzi were responsible.

Those photographers still on the spot, who had already been detained and corralled to one side of the crash scene by police, were loaded roughly into a police bus and taken to the cells, where they were given a humiliating strip search and internal examination in the hunt for hidden film. The beasts that had killed the beauty were under lock and key, and others would be rounded up in the next twenty-four hours to join them, said the authorities.

Unfortunately, there was a major flaw in this solution. A flaw that occurred again in the subsequent "solution" adopted by the police and judiciary: none of the real facts supported their case. Not that such mundane things as facts and truth would be permitted to deter the commander of the Criminal Brigade, Jean-Claude Mules, who was charged with investigating the night's events. Six years later this smugly arrogant functionary claims to have conducted the perfect investigation, but he patently supervised one of the most slipshod, tunnel-visioned and disturbing criminal investigations in the history of the French gendarmerie. Important evidence was rejected out of hand, and obvious leads were deliberately ignored.

From the outset, Commander Mules and his Criminal Brigade's reaction to any witness who disagreed with their version of events was uniform. They ignored the evidence and discredited the witness. First to fall foul of this bizarre official policy was a young motorcyclist called Eric Petel, who was driving along the Cours Albert Ier after midnight when he was overtaken by Diana's Mercedes. "The car was going quite fast, and after it passed me I heard a sort of implosion," said Petel. "As I had just bought the motorbike, I thought the noise may have come from my exhaust and that I had a problem there. So I slowed down, thinking the bike had gone funny. Then I heard a much louder noise: the sound of a car crashing at speed.

"Ahead I saw the Mercedes which had exploded head-on into a heavy concrete pillar in the center of the dual freeway. It had spun around and was facing back the way it had come. The horn was still blaring. I went to the car and saw a woman in the back. She had fallen against the seat in front and was bent over. I tried to ease her back and her head flopped back and I saw a little blood was coming from her nose and ear. That's weird, I thought. I know this person."

Petel said his first instinct was to call for help. "But I didn't have a mobile. I don't like them." He went instead to a public telephone, off the Place de l'Alma, and called the emergency services from there. Of the remarkable number of eyewitnesses, he was one of the very few who even attempted to raise the alarm.

François Levistre from Rouen in Normandy was interviewed by the Reuters Paris office four days after the crash. He and his wife Valerie were in Paris for a night out, and were driving into the Alma tunnel when he noticed lights approaching from behind in his rearview mirror. "I said to my wife that there must be a big shot behind us with a police escort. Then I went down into the tunnel and again in my rearview mirror I saw the car in the middle of the tunnel with a motorcycle on its left with two people on it which then swerved to the right directly in front of the car.

"As it swerved there was a flash of light. It was an explosion of light. Like a searchlight. But then I was heading out of the tunnel and heard, but did not see, the impact. I immediately pulled my car over to the curb but my wife said, 'Let's get out of here. It's a terrorist attack.' "

Lamentably, Levistre's evidence became tainted when he changed his story in a bid to make money. He claimed, in a story used by the *Sunday People*, that it was he who was responsible for the crash. He had swerved in front of the motorcycle, he said, and forced it into the path of the Mercedes. From the other evidence available, this version of events was just not possible, said police, who showed no hesitation in using this to discredit both Levistre's accounts of what happened—in spite of Valerie Levistre's assurance that the original version, given to the judiciary and the police, had been the true account, and could be trusted. It is certainly an account which ties in with various other witness statements, but does not complement the official version of events.

Brian Anderson, an American businessman from California, was traveling in a taxi and saw a motorcycle with two riders aboard pass the Mercedes on the left. "My attention was then drawn away until the cab came to a sudden stop and I saw an object in front of us, crossing over. Sparks were flying, there was dust, there was a lot of noise and it happened very quickly and the car came down and rested on its tires. In that instant the horn went off."

A forty-year-old British secretary, Brenda Wells, was returning home after a party and told police that as she neared the Alma tunnel she had been forced off the road by a motorcycle with two men on board traveling at high speed. "It was following a big car. After, in the tunnel, there were very strong lights, like flashes. I saw the big car had come off the road and I stopped. After that, five or six motorcycles arrived and people started taking photographs."

Thierry H., a fifty-nine-year-old Parisian engineer, who wished to remain anonymous, and Eric Lee, a chauffeur, also reported having seen the two-rider motorcycle aggressively and dangerously pursuing the Mercedes, at high speed, as it approached the tunnel.

One witness, who said he had not realized the significance of what he had seen until much later after reading reports of the Fiat Uno, was off-duty French policeman David Laurent. In June 1998 he made an official statement that he was driving toward the Alma tunnel when a white car sped past him. As Laurent neared the tunnel he again saw the car, which he recognized as a Fiat Uno, now creeping along very slowly. It had no reason to slow down but had come to a near standstill in the inside lane just before the tunnel entrance.

At that point there was no Mercedes in sight.

Laurent had driven past, leaving the Fiat Uno inching toward the tunnel. He said he believed the Fiat was waiting for another car. In retrospect, he said in his statement, it was quite possibly Princess Diana's Mercedes that it was waiting for.

A witness known as Gaelle L., who also wished to remain anonymous, told police that as she entered the tunnel from the opposite direction she heard a loud noise of screeching tires. "At that moment in the opposite lane, I saw a large car approaching at high speed. The car swerved to the left and to the right and crashed into the wall with its horn blaring. I should note that in front of this car there was another, smaller car. I think the vehicle was black, but I'm not sure." It must be pointed out that, under the dim French street lighting, it is sometimes difficult to differentiate between dark and light colors of cars.

Gaelle parked outside the tunnel and, joined by her boyfriend Benoit, who was traveling with her, jumped out of her car to flag down oncoming vehicles. Her call to the French fire department emergency number on a borrowed mobile phone was one of the first to be received.

Eyewitness Gary Dean stated that the Mercedes was traveling very fast before the tunnel, and gave off a whooshing noise as it entered the tunnel "as if the driver had hit the clutch but failed to change gear."

Two other witnesses, interviewed in the *Journal de Dimanche* on September 7, preferred to remain anonymous. One is quoted as saying, "The Mercedes was driving on the right hand, shortly before the entry to the tunnel, preceded by a dark-colored automobile, of which make I cannot say. This car clearly was attempting to force the Mercedes to brake. The driver of the Mercedes veered into the left-hand lane and then entered the tunnel."

The other witness, who was walking by the Seine, said he saw a Mercedes traveling behind another automobile. "I believe the reason why the Mercedes accelerated so suddenly was to try to veer into the left lane and pass that car."

These eleven witnesses between them provide all the available non-technical evidence on the actual crash, and the powerful thread of convincing circumstantial and hard evidence running through them is that a Fiat Uno and a two-passenger motorcycle combined to force the Mercedes off the road deliberately. Yet at no time during their two-year investigation did the police or judiciary consider this as a possible scenario. The fact that both the vehicles were driven from the scene immediately following the crash, and that the occupants of neither vehicle made an attempt to report the incident, offer assistance or subsequently turn to the Ritz Hotel for damages, did not, apparently, rouse police suspicions at all. That they were both in hiding could have suggested they had played a material role in the crash. But not to the Paris police.

As Commander Mules so succinctly explained, "If you start off with an investigation into an accident, one cannot add things that would only complicate the original hypothesis."

The first people to approach the Mercedes, after Eric Petel, were paparazzo Romuald Rat and his driver Stephane Darmon. They went ten meters past the wreckage, parked their motorcycle, a Honda 650, in the road and walked back. Darmon hung back because, he said later, he felt queasy. Romuald Rat seemed immune to such feelings. In a scene straight out of a Mad Max movie the hulking Rat, who had earlier frightened Diana outside Dodi's apartment, reached into the wreckage and touched her.

"She was alive," he said, "and rubbing her stomach. She was speaking English."

Possibly because of the Anglo-Saxon connotation of his name, a wave of revulsion swept around the world when he revealed that he had taken Diana's pulse by placing his fingers on her neck. He said later he had told her, in English, to stay cool and hold on, and that help would come. He claimed not to have taken pictures until the emergency services arrived, but this was a lie. Police, who confiscated his film, found his first four frames of the crash scene showed no other person or vehicle in the picture.

The next to arrive, Christian Martinez, had an even worse reputation than Rat. It is virtually impossible to find any of the paparazzi who have a good word to say for him. He is ruthless, mean-spirited and violent, they say. Martinez and Rat were to be central figures in some of the worst scrimmages and exchanges of abuse around the death scene, to the extent of preventing the first police to arrive from reaching the victims.

The first tussle involving the two of them took place outside the rear door of the Mercedes after Rat discovered Diana was still alive. Several photographers took part in the struggle with one another in an attempt to get the best vantage point from which to take pictures of the princess. Serge Arnal, David Odekerken and Serge Banamou were only seconds behind the early arrivals. They popped their flashguns at the broken bodies, and at the barely conscious princess, poking their cameras through the shattered windows and buckled doors. A couple contented themselves with photographing the wreckage.

By the time the paparazzi had begun their frenzy of picture-taking, Eric Petel had contacted the emergency services but was not certain they had understood the seriousness of the crash or the importance of its victim. He decided to go personally to the nearest police station to give them the full facts, face-to-face, so they would appreciate the gravity of the situation.

The emergency services say the first call they received was from photographer Serge Arnal, who called 112 at 12:32 A.M. He says he made the call before phoning his senior editor and dashing into the tunnel to take sixteen pictures. What is certain is that when Dr. Frédéric Mailliez, a doctor with SOS Médécin, arrived, the paparazzi were in full spate and shooting the car and its occupants from all angles. He had been driving in the opposite direction, on the way home from a party, when he saw the crash. He was the first to try to help the injured.

Said Mailliez, "The driver was dead and the back, male passenger was also dead. The front passenger had been hurled against the dashboard and windshield and the left side of his face had sustained most of the damage. It was ripped off and hanging loose. Even to a doctor it was a gruesome sight. The woman in the back seemed to be in the best shape. She looked pretty fine. I thought this woman had a chance." Amazingly, the doctor said that he did not recognize the princess.

Dr. Mailliez forced his way out, past the paparazzi, "who seemed to have taken all leave of their senses," and ran back to his car. Using his mobile phone he made two calls: one to confirm that two ambulances were on their way—"I told them there were two severely injured people"—and another to request the heavy cutting gear which would be needed to free Trevor Rees-Jones from the wreckage. Collecting what meager medical equipment he carried with him in his car, Dr. Mailliez ran back to the Mercedes to give first aid to the injured woman.

In the time he had been away, two off-duty volunteer firemen who had also been driving in the opposite direction had stopped to help. Damien Dalby and Sébastien Pennequin had gone to the aid of the trapped bodyguard, holding his bloody head in their hands to help him breathe.

Dr. Mailliez said there was very little he could do for Diana. Through the open back door he was able to tilt her head back slightly and clear her upper respiratory passage and put an oxygen mask over her nose and mouth. "I sought to unblock her trachea and stop her tongue blocking the esophagus. This seemed to ease her breathing and made her more animated," he said.

The princess was only semiconscious but talking, although the doctor said he could not understand what she was saying. "While I was inside the car giving assistance to Princess Diana, I was aware of a lot of flashes, a lot of people taking a lot of pictures of myself and the princess."

The first police arrived at 12:30 A.M., just before the fire brigade, and they too had to push their way through the paparazzi who were snapping the car from every angle, including taking pictures of the doctor treating Diana. Experts who examined the photographs later revealed that several had been taken with the lenses less than four-and-a-half-feet from the princess's face. One, by Serge Arnal, was taken just four feet away while Dr. Mailliez was treating her. One observer, Mark Butt, said, "They were going for close shots, and then back out. They did get rather close and that's what bothered me. To see how close they were getting with their huge lenses, right on top of them, within fifty or sixty centimeters."

Officers Lino Gagliardone and Sebastian Dorzee were patroling along the Cours Albert Ier when they were told of the accident by passers-by. They parked their patrol car at the entrance to the tunnel and used their radio to summon reinforcements.

Gagliardone tried, with little success, to hold back the paparazzi while Dorzee checked the condition of the car's occupants and reported back to the local station. He was able to tell them that the princess was still alive, but bleeding from the nose and from a substantial wound on her forehead. She was still talking—mumbling rather—and he thought she said, "My God" when she saw Dodi's body. "She was moving slightly and her eyes were open. She was in pain, I think. She turned her head toward the front of the car and saw the driver. I think she understood better, then, what had happened. She became quite agitated. Then she looked at me and closed her eyes and let her head rest back."

By the time Eric Petel walked into the local police station and was talking to the desk officer, his information had already preceded him. Said Petel, "I told the policeman on the desk, 'Quick, quick. You have to call the emergency services. Lady Di has had a crash. She's had an accident, and you must call for an ambulance straight away.'

"The cop said, 'Are you joking?'

"I told him no, and that I was serious. I grabbed one of the files from his desk and threw it on the floor, to try and get his full attention, and told him, 'You've got to do something.'

"He called another cop and they tried to calm me. But the more they tried to calm me the more upset I became. They didn't seem to understand. 'You must do something,' I shouted. So they did. They put me in handcuffs."

At the Alma tunnel the situation was still chaotic. Said officer Gagliardone, "The photographers were virulent, objectionable and pushy, continuing to take photos and willfully obstructing an officer from assisting the victims."

Clifford Gooroovadoo, a limousine driver who had been waiting for his clients in the Place de l'Alma, had rushed to the crash scene. "Four or five men were already taking photographs around the wrecked Mercedes," he said. "It was obvious the four occupants were wounded. There was blood; their bodies were sprawled every which way inside the Mercedes. Yet these men photographed the car and the wounded from every angle. Seeing this spectacle I shouted, 'Is that all you can do instead of calling for help?'

"The passenger in front, who was trying to move, seemed to have had his mouth and tongue ripped off. I held up his head and told him not to move, to await help.

"I saw a blonde head moving in the back and someone said, 'That's Lady Di.' So I repeated the same words to this young woman in English. Lady Di tried to speak. She opened her mouth to tell me something, but no sound came out. She was bleeding from the forehead and was trying to get up. The photographers never stopped taking pictures. Romuald Rat was particularly manic at that time, moving around in all directions and arguing with Christian Martinez."

These scenes, ugly as they were, would soon become even worse. Two teams of firemen had arrived in vehicles 94 and 100 at 12:32 A.M., and the officer in charge, Sergeant Xavier Gourmelon, had evaluated the position. His main priority, he decided, was to cut the roof wreckage from the Mercedes to permit them to extract Trevor Rees-Jones, who appeared to everyone to be the most severely injured of the two casualties. He was standing next to Princess Diana and heard her say, "My God, what's happened," and saw her move her left arm and legs.

Gagliardone was, meanwhile, coming under increasingly hostile abuse from the paparazzi, who resented being told to move away to give the firemen room to work. One photographer told him, "If you had been in Bosnia you would not take it so tragically."

Christian Martinez snarled, "You make me sick. Let me do my job. In Sarajevo the police at least let us work."

One of the first senior officials to be dispatched to the scene was Madame Maude Coujard, the duty prosecutor. When someone dies violently in France, the first to be informed is the prosecution office, which in Paris is in the Palais de Justice. They, in turn, dispatch a prosecutor to the scene. Wearing a black leather jacket and jeans, Maude Coujard, a woman in her early thirties, was driven to the crash scene by her husband on their BMW motorcycle. She would oversee the French investigation into the crash, and appoint other officials and judges.

Her first on-the-spot decision was to place the case in the hands of the Criminal Brigade, the judicial police who investigate criminal and terrorist cases as well as sudden and inexplicable death. Its chief, Commander Jean-Claude Mules, placed his most trusted senior officer, Martine Monteil, in command. She was the first female head of the Brigade, having been appointed in 1996.

The duty judge, Hervé Stephan, had also been ordered to the scene that night, but it would be two full days before Madame Coujard would appoint him the senior judge to conduct the full investigation into the crash.

Paris chief of police Philippe Massoni had been informed and was on his way to the crash site. He had already conferred with minister of the interior Jean-Pierre Chevènement who was in touch with the British ambassador Sir Michael Jay. The foreign minister and the Elysée Palace had also been fully briefed.

From Commander Mules's subsequent comments, leaked accounts at the time and since, and from the British government's absolute refusal then to initiate an inquest or official inquiry into the deaths, the uppermost requirement at the very outset, by all parties involved, was that the crash be declared an accident; more specifically, nobody should believe that it had been deliberately engineered. The police and politicians were looking for an easily acceptable, uncomplicated explanation; fortunately for them, one readily and forcefully presented itself to anyone arriving at the Alma tunnel: the outrageous and unpalatable behavior of the paparazzi.

Soon after Martine Monteil's arrival, and following consultation with prosecutor Maude Coujard and a radio discussion with Commander Mules and the interior minister, it was decided at this very early stage of the investigation to place the sole blame for the accident on the paparazzi. They had clearly harassed the princess and her driver to the extent of forcing them off the road, it was said. That the evidence from virtually all the available eyewitnesses contradicted this version did not deter them from pursuing this official, and convenient, snap judgment. Romuald Rat, Stéphane Darmon, Christian Martinez, Jacques Langevin, Serge Arnol, Laslo Veres and Nikola Arsov were herded away from the crash by police reinforcements and taken into custody.

The Paris prosecution department would ask for an inquiry to be opened against the above named, and others arrested later, for failing to give assistance to persons in danger, and against unnamed persons for homicide and involuntary injury. The inquiry would clarify the context in which the photographers had followed the Mercedes in which Dodi and Diana were traveling, and the effect of their presence on the behavior of the driver of the vehicle immediately before the accident. In addition, the preliminary investigation file had to identify and examine the attitude adopted by these same photographers in the moments which immediately preceded the accident.

Sergeant Gourmelon had designated one of his ninety-five-strong team, Philippe Boyer, to take over from Dr. Mailliez and look after Princess Diana until the emergency service *Service d'Aide Médicale Urgente* (SAMU) arrived. Boyer attached a surgical collar around her neck. He would stay with her until the SAMU physicians took over. Two other firemen were assigned to help Trevor Rees-Jones. They held his head up from the dashboard to free his breathing, and administered oxygen before they also attached a cervical collar to his neck in case of spinal damage.

At 12:44 A.M. the "can opener" or *camion de dés-*

incarcération arrived, under the command of Armand Forge. Within moments, on Gourmelon's instructions, he had spotlights focused on the wreckage and began cutting the roof away.

By now Dr. Jean-Marc Martino, a resuscitation specialist with the SAMU rescue team, had taken over attending to Diana. A completely separate team, led by Dr. Le Hote, was concentrating on Trevor Rees-Jones, who was still believed to be the more seriously injured of the two casualties. Dr. Martino attached a drip to Diana's arm to sedate her, as she was still agitated and crying out. He said she was confused and incoherent. When the roof had been removed, he personally supervised the firemen and medics who hoisted her slim body from the rear of the Mercedes onto a stretcher. They took great care lifting her out as she was partly wedged on the floor, between the back seat and the passenger seat in front.

Dr. Martino judged her state as "severe but not critical" and he noted that she was still speaking, though not clearly. But as she was being transferred onto the stretcher, the princess went into cardiac arrest, and immediately the full seriousness of her condition started to become apparent. Dr. Martino gave her respiratory ventilation by inserting a narrow tracheal tube down her throat, and administered heart massage. All this took place on the stretcher by the roadside. Eventually he managed to revive her and immediately instructed ambulance driver Michel Massebeuf to transfer her stretcher to one of the waiting ambulances, where he continued to treat her. The interior of the ambulance was like a miniature emergency center—designed to be far more capable of treating patients and dealing with emergencies than their British equivalent.

It was then nearly 1:30 A.M.

The bodies of Henri Paul and Dodi Fayed had already been removed and laid on the road. Medics worked for thirty minutes, giving external heart massage in an attempt to resuscitate Dodi, but it was hopeless. The two corpses were eventually covered with blue plastic sheets, though they would not be declared dead until later.

Dr. Marc Le Jay, in charge of the unit's radio and telephone communications, had been told very soon after his arrival that the princess and her bodyguard were to be sent to the Pitié-Salpêtrière hospital. It was not the closest hospital, but the best equipped unit for this kind of trauma, he had been advised. This in itself was odd, as no one at this stage was aware of the full extent of their injuries. But in the end it would not make much difference to Diana. Astonishingly the ambulance in which she was traveling would not reach the emergency gates of the hospital—four miles away—until 2:06 A.M., one hour and forty-six minutes after the crash. By that time it was too late to save her; at 1:30 A.M. there still seemed to be hope.

There was not much hope, though, for Eric Petel. He was now being interviewed by a third policeman. "I tried to tell him what I had seen, but he kept asking about paparazzi," he said. This would seem to indicate that in the police station there was sufficient information being radioed in for them to know how the paparazzi were behaving, and even to know that charges against them were being considered. "I told him that there were no paparazzi present when the car crashed, but it didn't seem to be the right story. Soon after this I was bundled into a police van, still in handcuffs, and taken to Criminal Brigade headquarters on the Quai des Orfèvres.

"I couldn't work out what was happening. All I had done was come to warn them about a car accident involving a famous person, and now they were taking me away in handcuffs. I told them again and again exactly what I had seen and heard, and a very senior police officer in brigade headquarters told me, 'That's not how it happened.'

" 'But I was there,' I told him.

"It would be best, he said, if I did not make myself known to the press. It felt and sounded very much like a threat. He kept telling me that the crash could not have happened in the way I had described. What they wanted, exactly, they didn't say. It was as if I hadn't been there and had seen nothing."

That day the police briefed the press that Eric Petel could not be trusted. He was a liar, they said. Jean Durrieux, chief reporter of *Paris Match*, said, "I spoke to Petel three days later. I know he went to the police station and that he was interrogated by the Criminal Brigade. By suppressing Petel's evidence the French police could blame the photographers."

The investigating judge did not interview Petel until seven months after the crash, and asked the Criminal Brigade for a copy of the original statement he had made to the police. The Brigade reported that they could not find the original statement, and it has never been produced. Initially they claimed that he had never even attempted to call the emergency services. Then they admitted that he had made the call, but had not spoken clearly enough. The recording showed that Petel had told the emergency operator that he was speaking from Armand Marceau and not Alma Marceau, the subway station next to the tunnel, they said. No such place as Armand Marceau exists.

THIRTEEN

There exist several conspiracy theories which suggest that the ambulance taking Diana from the crash scene to hospital deliberately dawdled, so that by the time she reached the operating theater, and could be dealt with by skilled surgeons, her death was already assured. The truth, I am convinced, is far simpler.

The French bungled the rescue operation, as they would bungle the police investigation which followed, and allowed a "play-it-by-the-book" medical team, lacking both the initiative and ingenuity to dictate the best sequence of care for the princess's urgent needs, to control her vital early treatment. Their true dedication, it appeared, was in following the rigid French emergency service procedures, rather than acting in Diana's best interests. There was also the added complication of her heart having twice stopped beating during the rescue mission.

It was 1:30 A.M. when the French emergency rescue vehicle, or mobile surgery unit—it would be totally misleading to call it simply an ambulance—pulled away from the Alma tunnel with its escort of two police cars and two police motorcyclists. It has been argued by many doctors in Britain and the United States that had Diana been driven at high speed to the nearest hospital and undergone surgery within thirty minutes of the crash taking place, she might well have survived. As it was, the emergency vehicle traveled so slowly that the short journey took thirty-six minutes to complete—an average speed of seven miles per hour. Driver Michel Massebeuf explained later that the reason for going so slowly was to prevent passage over bumpy road surfaces from aggravating the patient's condition.

As they were crossing the Austerlitz bridge, Diana's heart appeared to have stopped beating for the second time, her blood pressure became dangerously low and Dr. Jean-Marc Martino ordered the convoy to stop. By now they had already passed two major hospitals and were outside the botanical gardens, less than half a mile from Pitié-Salpêtrière. Many might have been tempted to make the thirty-second dash to the waiting operating theater and state-of-the-art medical equipment at the surgeons' disposal, particularly as the SAMU vehicle was not equipped to perform major surgery. But Dr. Martino, using his temporary authority, opted to deal with the emergency himself. This added a further, and some would argue later, an unnecessary ten minutes to the journey. Again he applied external heart massage, and injected a large dose of adrenaline directly into the heart, before ordering Massebeuf to drive on.

Senior politicians, police and one diplomat—British ambassador Sir Michael Jay—were already gathered at the entrance to the hospital. Paris police chief Philippe Massoni, who had driven another route from the crash scene, was also there, and they were all becoming highly concerned at the non-arrival of the princess. No one could explain, or justify, the seemingly interminable delay. Massoni admitted afterward that he genuinely believed at one stage that the emergency convoy might even have got lost! This could explain why Jean-Pierre Chevènement, the interior minister, looked so patently anxious as he strove to reassure Sir Michael that the princess would arrive shortly.

When the mobile emergency unit did finally arrive, at 2:06 A.M., the hospital's head of intensive care Professor Bruno Riou was standing by to take over responsibility for Diana's medical treatment. Yet inexplicably, and despite the flow of radio data from the emergency SAMU team highlighting two cardiac arrests in little over thirty minutes, there was no specialist heart surgeon on standby. Nor did the medical team suggest having a heart–lung bypass machine available, which is used to keep patients alive during major heart surgery or transplant operations. Diana was unconscious when she arrived, and receiving artificial respiration, but her heart was still beating at this point. X-rays revealed both massive internal hemorrhaging and appalling internal injuries.

The princess was being drained of the blood, which had spilled into her chest area, when she suffered a further cardiac arrest at 2:10 A.M. It was Professor Bruno who ordered duty surgeon Maniel

Daloman to open her chest on the right side while he applied external heart massage. Not until the operation was well under way did Professor Alain Pavie, a belatedly summoned specialist heart surgeon, arrive to take charge. Having quickly confirmed that the massive internal bleeding was coming from a ruptured pulmonary vein—a major link between the heart and the lungs—Pavie sutured the 2.5-centimeter split while heart massage continued to be administered. Throughout the operation a nurse was giving constant injections of adrenaline to keep Diana's heart going. A staggering total of 150 5ml doses were injected.

But no cardiac activity could be re-established.

At 3 A.M., Professor Pavie extended the original incision and began massaging the heart by hand. This procedure was explained to the interior minister and Sir Michael at 3:30 A.M. by Professor Bruno Riou, who warned them that the diagnosis was pessimistic. After all other attempts to produce a spontaneous heart rhythm had failed, Professor Pavia ordered electric shock therapy in a last-ditch effort to restart the princess's heart. Time after time massive electrical charges were arced between the hand-held terminals pressed on her chest. But her heart failed to respond.

Finally, and by mutual consent, all attempts at resuscitation were abandoned, and the princess was declared dead at 4 A.M.

The last rites were administered by Roman Catholic priest Father Clochard-Bossuet, who anointed Diana with holy oil.

An official bulletin, signed by Professors Riou and Pavie, stated:

The Princess of Wales was the victim of a high-speed car crash tonight in Paris. She was immediately taken by the Paris SAMU emergency services which carried out initial resuscitation.

On her arrival at Pitié-Salpêtrière hospital, she had massive chest injuries and hemorrhaging, followed rapidly by cardiac arrest.

An emergency thoracotomy revealed a major wound on the left pulmonary vein.

Despite closing this wound and two hours of external and internal cardiac massage, circulation could not be re-established and death occurred at 4 o'clock in the morning.

Diana had also sustained a broken arm and had an unusual puncture wound in her hip, for which no explanation has ever been given.

Dr. Patrick Goldstein, vice-president of SAMU said, "We can't do the impossible. Diana had no chance of making it. The accident was too violent. The internal injuries she suffered were incompatible with life." Criticism and outright condemnation of the French emergency medical system poured in from around the world, however—the consensus being that if the princess had been transferred to hospital sooner, then she might have survived. The French counterclaimed that it was exceptional for anyone with such injuries as the princess had suffered even to reach the hospital alive.

American surgeons then reminded them that President Ronald Reagan's pulmonary artery had been torn by an assassin's bullet in 1981 and that he had survived, in his seventies, because of the speed with which the Secret Service rushed him to hospital.

No doubt it is a debate that will continue for years to come.

What is not in dispute is that Princess Diana's heart was actually knocked sideways, several inches, by the violence of the impact, and that this tore her pulmonary vein which caused her to bleed to death. One rumor which began circulating immediately after her death was that blood tests, which showed that the princess was pregnant, were removed from the hospital laboratory later that day. This was vehemently denied by the hospital, and their public affairs department went as far as issuing a press statement denying that blood samples had ever been taken from the princess.

"She would have needed an awful lot of blood transfusions to keep her alive," said one leading trauma surgeon, however. "And they did that without typing or testing her blood in any way? Nonsense!" In fact, the hospital confirmed she had received seven liters of blood. So why the denials that her blood was tested?

The public announcement of Diana's death was made at 5:45 A.M. by Sir Michael Jay. By this time, photographs of Diana receiving treatment inside the wrecked Mercedes had already been electronically distributed around the world.

One agency, Laurent Sola, had photos scanned into its computer to be e-mailed internationally. These were already attracting offers totaling over £1 million from England alone. But after being told that the princess was dead, Laurent Sola himself scrapped all deals in the making and withdrew the photos from sale. It took him only a moment, he said, to make this costly decision. "There was never a question we would try to cash in on this tragic situation," he said. He ordered his staff to remove all traces of the photos from the computer, and arranged to hand over the unused photos to the British Embassy to be handed to the families of the victims.

Other picture agencies in Paris, which had received paparazzi photos from the crash site, showing the injured and dead, also withdrew them from the market and, in the end, not one questionable photograph was sold.

Earlier, while Diana was still alive and before the crash victims were cut free, the first harrowing calls were being made to the victims' relatives. One of the first was to Mohamed Al Fayed.

The "decoys"—the Range Rover driven by Philippe Dourneau and carrying Kez Wingfield, and the Mercedes driven by Jean-Francis Musa—had taken a more direct route to Dodi's apartment, but had become caught up in the gridlock of traffic which rapidly built up after the crash. When they finally reached the rue Arsène Houssaye, Kez went up to the apartment and tried to contact Trevor Rees-Jones on the land line, having previously failed to get him using his mobile. He believed then that Dodi had probably decided to go into a nightclub and that this was the cause of their non-arrival. In the street below the drivers Dourneau and Musa mingled with a small group of waiting journalists, and were close by when one of them received a call about the crash from a colleague. The two drivers alerted Kez that Dodi's car had been involved in an accident, before jumping into the Range Rover and driving as close as they could get to the Alma tunnel.

Kez telephoned the bare information to the London operations desk, and urged Philippe Dourneau to get as close to the crash scene as possible on foot and try to get more details. When he did, the news was devastating. Dodi was dead, he told Kez. Henri Paul and Trevor Rees-Jones were dead too. Diana had hurt her legs but seemed OK.

Kez passed the awful news directly to Mohamed Al Fayed's chief of personal security, Paul Handley-Greaves, in London. At 1:30 A.M., the lights snapped on in Barrow Green Court, the Surrey farmhouse home of the Harrods chairman, who listened to Handley-Greaves gently breaking the news that his beloved eldest son, Dodi, was dead, and that Princess Diana could be dying.

Bodyguards drove the grief-stricken tycoon the twenty miles to Gatwick airport, where his private helicopter was waiting for him on the tarmac. Within minutes it had taken off for Paris.

At the same time, a telephone call from the switchboard at Buckingham Palace—alerted by the Foreign Office—awakened Prince Charles, who was holidaying with his sons in a shooting lodge in the grounds of gloomy Balmoral Castle. Prince Charles later told friends that he listened with mounting horror and then called his mother who, with Prince Philip and the rest of the court hangers-on, was spending her traditional summer holiday at Balmoral.

Before dawn, ashen-faced, Charles went to see his mother and told her it was his intention to fly to Paris at first light. He intended bringing home the body of his former wife aboard an aircraft of the Queen's Flight. The Queen said it was not a good idea, and it wasn't until after breakfast, in a conference with courtiers during which Charles remained adamant that he was leaving for Paris, that she finally relented—and only then after an unusually courageous equerry had asked, "Would you prefer, ma'am, that the body of the Princess of Wales be brought home in a Harrods van?"

In Paris, Kez Wingfield and the Ritz Hotel's acting manager Claude Roulet drove to Le Bourget airport in the northern suburbs of the city, and arrived at 4:55 A.M. just as the Harrods helicopter arrived hovering overhead. It touched down as the Range Rover and Al Fayed's Mercedes drew to a stop.

At that exact moment Kez Wingfield took a call from the British Consulate.

"Princess Diana is dead."

When Al Fayed, flanked by two bodyguards, stepped from the helicopter, Kez, who had never touched his boss before, put his arm around his shoulders and said, "I'm sorry for your loss, sir, but I have some more bad news for you."

"The princess?"

"I'm afraid they're all dead."

As they drove back into the center of Paris, Kez, in the front of Al Fayed's car, heard him suddenly erupt, "I hope the British government is satisfied now."

"Nobody could have wished this, sir," gasped a shocked Wingfield, but Al Fayed had slumped in his seat, quite inconsolable, and did not reply.

They arrived at the hospital front entrance shortly before the official announcement was made that Princess Diana was dead.

Mohamed Al Fayed did not go into the hospital, but was met, on the entrance steps, by an official. He did not, as he would claim later, view Princess Diana's body, and did not talk to a nurse who, he would later announce, had given him the princess's last words. Those were the tycoon's private fantasies, and did not take place. It is indisputable that the billionaire's pathetic lies, probably intended to enhance the importance of his minor role in events, caused a great deal of hurt to Diana's children and others, and they will find it very hard to forgive his behavior. But at the time he was uncharacteristically subdued. When the official showed them around to the morgue, where a hearse was waiting, they had to wait while the keys were found to let them in. Al Fayed simply stood there, deep in shock, saying nothing.

There was some good news from the hospital official. Trevor Rees-Jones was in poor shape, but he was alive. Kez telephoned this news to the Ritz to be relayed to London and Trevor's family.

Including the time it took to claim Dodi's body, Al Fayed was at the hospital for less than ten minutes. Their convoy then returned to the airport, via Dodi's apartment where they collected Diana's luggage which had already been packed.

As the Harrods helicopter carrying Dodi's body back to England took off from Le Bourget airport, a different kind of machine entirely was being driven down the Alma tunnel.

Incredibly, the Criminal Brigade had ordered that the municipal street cleaner be sent through the tunnel. Using mechanical scouring brushes, and spraying strong detergent, disinfectant and water, the cumbersome green machine made two passes over the section of road where Diana had died. Any forensic evidence that might have been available was destroyed in the deliberate clean-up. Or was it the start of the cover-up? Had this been a normal accident, involving a visiting VIP, the road would have remained closed for at least twenty-four hours so that a thorough, inch by inch, examination could be made. There were only three crash-scene experts at that time at police headquarters in Paris. By the time one of them could be found to send to the Alma tunnel, the roadsweeper had been through and done its damage.

Six hours after the crash, while the Harrods helicopter was still only half way across the channel, the tunnel was fully reopened to traffic. The only clue to a major crash having taken place there was a large chunk of concrete missing from the base of the thirteenth pillar. Said Christopher Dickey, *Newsweek*'s Paris correspondent, "I went there at seven o'clock to view the scene, and was stunned to find it already reopened. I would have thought that for an incident of that magnitude, involving the death of such a famous individual, the police might have kept it closed for days in their search for evidence."

The Paris traffic police had already made a cursory examination of the site earlier, but their report would prove to be of academic interest only. Martine Monteil, in charge of the Criminal Brigade investigation, announced that she had no interest in reading any report, factual, technical or speculative, from the traffic police. There was never any consultation or cooperation between the two police departments. Nor was the traffic department asked by Judge Stephan to submit a report to his inquiry.

Equally inexplicable is the Criminal Brigade's blatant rejection of an immediate offer of help from Mercedes-Benz, which manufactures the Mercedes, to send engineers to examine the wrecked car and assess possible causes of the crash and its condition and behavior leading up to impact. It is incontestable that Mercedes-Benz would have provided the best assessment possible.

It was to be a morning of unusual decisions. One of the most controversial was the priority command from London to perform a partial embalming of Diana's body, from the waist up, before an autopsy was undertaken. The order was passed on to French authorities by Sir Michael Jay on behalf of Prince Charles's St. James's Palace office. Whether these orders originated from the prince himself or from some nameless, faceless member of the Establishment is not known. Either way, they did not come from Diana's next of kin, making the orders illegal under French law—not that the French complained at the time. They seemed perfectly willing to cave in under the combined diplomatic and royal pressure. They also turned a blind eye to the breaking of another French law, which bans embalming if a postmortem is to be carried out, because the formaldehyde corrupts some toxicological tests.

One of these susceptible tests is for pregnancy.

The only comment from the French police came six years after the event, from Commander Mules. "The decision was taken by a higher authority than myself, before the body was released."

The partial embalming presumably achieved what it was intended to achieve. It certainly resulted in two outcomes. It limited the chances of there being a successful, full autopsy in either France or England, and it made it difficult to confirm if Diana had been pregnant at the time of her death.

One of the doctors who carried out the procedure, Professor Dominique Lecomte, still maintains that she behaved correctly. "We did nothing wrong," she says. Because of the embalming, she and the other forensic pathologist Professor Andre Lienhart did not carry out a full autopsy. The professors merely confirmed the nature of the injuries which caused Diana's death.

Full notes, including an account of the embalming and the pathologists' observations, were handed to French authorities, but were not included in the report to Judge Stephan's inquiry. A decision was taken at the highest level to suppress this part of the medical report because, according to police leaks, Diana was pregnant and the evidence was deliberately concealed to save the princess's family embarrassment.

Other leaks claimed that a quantity of cocaine was discovered, by police, in the back of the Mercedes, and that it was evidence of the victims' use of this drug that was suppressed to save embarrassment.

Whatever the truth, embalming destroyed forever any positive evidence which would have revealed, beyond any doubt, if Diana was expecting a baby when she died.

According to Robert Thompson, an assistant at the Hammersmith and Fulham Mortuary in West London where an autopsy on Diana's body was later performed, "There had been some wadding inserted into the body. I presume it had been soaked in formaldehyde or formalin, because I could get that smell." When the mortuary blood-test results came through, they showed no indication of any alcohol in Diana's body, even though Thompson said that her stomach contents smelled strongly of alcohol. "It permeated the room," he said. "Indeed it was so strong that it forced me to step back a pace. Most of the others reacted to the smell. This leads me to the conclusion that there had been a deliberate attempt to cover up a potentially embarrassing situation."

Glasgow University Professor Peter Vanezis, a former London police pathologist, said, "Nobody should be embalmed before a postmortem. There is no good reason why this should have been done in the case of the princess."

According to Robert Thompson, at one point during the autopsy, forensic pathologist Dr. Chapman announced that Diana wasn't pregnant. But he did not himself see the evidence for this remark. "Another person, who was present, just as categorically told me that the princess was expecting a baby when she died."

Confirmation of this came after six years from highly rated *Daily Mail* journalist Sue Reid, who in December 2003 quoted a source, who wished to remain anonymous, saying that, in the days before she joined Dodi on holiday, Diana went to a leading London hospital to undergo a pregnancy scan. "Of course, at the time it was kept incredibly quiet," said the source. "The princess might have been divorced, but the idea of the mother of the future king becoming a single mother was too controversial to contemplate."

Possibly the last word on the pregnancy issue goes to Diana's self-confessed best friend Rosa Monckton, who claimed the princess had menstruated only a week before the crash, while they were holidaying together on a boat in Greece.

So that's that. Or is it?

According to ex-British spy Richard Tomlinson, Rosa's brother, the Honorable Anthony Leopold Colyer Monckton, a sometime diplomat, was a serving officer in MI6. In his book, published in Moscow in 2001, Tomlinson alleges that Rosa's husband, Dominic Lawson, provided journalistic cover for MI6 officers while he was editor of the *Spectator.* It was claimed that Lawson, son of the Tory Chancellor and brother of famous British cook Nigella Lawson, was on MI6's books in the early 1990s and provided cover for an agent named Spencer, who was put on the case of a young Russian diplomat, Pluton Obukhov, in Tallinn, the capital of Estonia.

In an excerpt from Tomlinson's book published in *Pravda,* it was revealed that Spencer, returning from a visit to Information Operations, which deals with the British media to arrange bogus journalistic credentials, remarked, "Flippin' outrageous. They've got the editor of the *Spectator* magazine on the books. He's called 'smallbrow'. He's agreed to let me go out to Tallinn undercover as a freelancer for his magazine. The only condition is that I have to write an article which he'll publish if he likes it. The cheeky bastard wants a story courtesy of the taxpayer."

Allegations that Lawson, who was editor of the *Spectator* from 1990–95 before becoming editor of the *Sunday Telegraph*, had connections with MI6 were also made in parliament, but he has always denied ever having been their agent.

Paris-based journalist Jane Tawbase headed a *EuroBusiness* investigation into Rosa Monckton and Lawson. She wrote, "Rosa Monckton, a generation older, made an odd friend for the often unhappy princess. A svelte sophisticate and a wealthy working woman, her first relationships and loyalties lay, almost from when she was born, with the Queen. She was a regular visitor to the royal household all her life and was, for that reason, more given to loyalty to the crown than to an unhappy and disruptive outsider, one who was seriously damaging the public image of the royal family."

When examined more closely, the friendship between Diana and Rosa, as Jane Tawbase observes, is an unnatural one: the older, very cerebral and refined woman of the world compared with a keep-fit fashion goddess whose pleasures were shopping and disco music. Tawbase poses two questions in her article. First, "whether Rosa Monckton introduced her brother to the princess and whether he was part of the MI6 operation. It was almost unthinkable that he was not," she says.

Second, "did MI6 ask Rosa Monckton to do the key job of moving into the princess's inner circle and become her confidante? It would certainly have made the job easier."

Tomlinson offers detailed evidence to support his claim about Rosa's brother, and if correct, it would make Anthony one of a long line of spies. Anthony and Rosa's grandfather worked for Edward VIII and kept a close eye on him on behalf of the security services throughout the abdication and beyond. "It would indeed be ironic," concludes Jane Tawbase, "if history had repeated itself and Rosa Monckton performed the same role for MI6 for Princess Diana."

How terribly convenient it would have been to have a conduit to the woman to whom Diana told everything, and to whom she would pour out her heart almost every night. In this scenario it would not be surprising for Rosa Monckton to declare that Diana was not pregnant when she died. In the words of another celebrity witness, "She would say that, wouldn't she?" After all, the reason for MI6 being involved in the murder was the abhorrent belief that she was expecting a Muslim child. If they killed to prevent it happening, surely they would go to great lengths afterward to prevent news of it getting out.

The conviction among the Establishment courtiers and their MI6 chums, before her death, was that Diana was pregnant. That is all that matters. Whether she was or not is now immaterial to the action that this belief helped to trigger.

The Queen's Flight carrying Prince Charles, Diana's two sisters—Lady Jane Fellowes and Lady Sarah McCorquodale—and a small group of aides and servants, landed in Paris shortly after 5 P.M. They were driven directly to the Pitié-Salpêtrière hospital, Charles traveling with Sir Michael Jay in a silver-gray Jaguar bearing the royal standard.

They arrived at 6 P.M. and were taken to the second floor to the room where Diana's body was laid out. She was wearing a black dress and held the ivory rosary beads given to her by Mother Teresa. Her hair had been washed and blow-dried. Paul Burrell was already there, and he, Prince Charles and the two sisters stood quietly around the body for several minutes. Shortly afterward, Diana's body was placed in a double coffin—a gray casket with a window, in accordance with French customs regulations, inside an oak coffin.

On the Queen's Flight BAE 146 taking the body back to RAF Northolt, Prince Charles invited Burrell to join the main group. Burrell had flown out by scheduled flights early that morning to visit the hospital and pick up Diana's effects from the Ritz Hotel. He had been advised there that all the Princess's things had already been taken back to England by Mohamed Al Fayed and would be forwarded to Kensington Palace.

At RAF Northolt, eight men removed the coffin from the aircraft's hold, covered it with the royal standard and transferred it to a waiting hearse. Diana's body still had many miles to travel, but her lover, Dodi, in accordance with the Muslim faith, had already been buried before sunset in the warm, English earth of a private cemetery in Surrey.

Charles flew on to Balmoral to be with his sons, and Jane Fellowes, Sarah McCorquodale and Paul Burrell followed the hearse to a London undertaker where the princess's personal doctor, Dr. Peter Wheeler, was waiting. He explained that an autopsy would now have to be performed in accordance with British law before Diana's coffin could be taken to lie in state in the Chapel Royal at St. James's Palace. Any autopsy done in Paris would not count. The autopsy was performed in Hammersmith and Fulham Mortuary in West London by the then coroner to the Queen's household, Dr. John Burton, and his deputy, Dr. Michael Burgess, the current coroner.

As long ago as 2000, a memorandum prepared by French pathologists Professors Lecomte and Lienhart, who handled the embalming in Paris, suggests that British authorities, including the royal coroner Dr. Burton, had interceded to conceal some aspects of the official British autopsy. The two French doctors were in London in June 1998, where they met with coroners Burton and Burgess, forensic pathologist Dr. Chapman, and Scotland Yard superintendent Jeffrey Rees. They were given copies of the English autopsy report on Princess Diana, but, according to their contemporaneous notes on the meeting, were told that the document was provided for their "private and personal use," and that it should not be included in the formal file of Judge Stephan, which would have become automatically available to solicitors representing other interested parties in the French probe.

This suppression of the Lecomte–Lienhart memorandum raised serious questions about the legitimacy of the "official" autopsy of the Princess of Wales, including questions that arose at the time of her death as to whether she was pregnant.

FOURTEEN

Twenty-four hours after the crash, two incidents took place at two separate addresses in London which bore a remarkable similarity to each other.

At 3 A.M., Lionel Cherruault, a London-based photojournalist, was woken at his home in Mobray Road by his wife's screams. She had looked downstairs and seen that the front door was wide open. The police were called and Cherruault discovered, on checking his studio, that they had been robbed. His car had been moved and his wife's car stolen while they and their daughter had been asleep. The only thefts from the house were computer discs and electronic equipment used for storing and transmitting photographs. The discs contained a vast library of royal pictures, and were the main targets.

The previous morning, just after the crash in Paris, Cherruault had been offered photographs of the tunnel crash—but the deal collapsed after

Diana died. Even the police admitted it was no ordinary burglary. Cash, credit cards and jewelry were in full view when the computer equipment was stolen, but had not been touched. Expensive cameras and lenses were also ignored. "They had shut down the computers and actually removed all the hard drives," said Lionel Cherruault. "The next day, a man came to see me wearing a gray suit. He also had gray hair. He told me I had been targeted, not burgled, and hinted at government involvement. He said, 'You can call them what you like—MI5, MI6, MI7, MI9, Special Branch or local henchmen—anything you like. But that person who came to your house had a key into your house and knew exactly where to go. But not to worry, your lives weren't in any danger.' "

Three hours earlier, and a few miles away in North London, Darryn Paul Lyons's photo laboratory was also broken into by mysterious raiders. By 3 A.M. on August 31 he had received crash photos, sent electronically from Paris by computer, from Laurent Sola, following a phone call shortly after 12:30 A.M. High-resolution photos were received and Lyons, who runs Big Pictures photo agency, was negotiating deals with British and American outlets. The deals were called off after Sola telephoned with news of Diana's death.

The following night between 11 P.M., August 31 and 12:30 A.M., September 1, the power to Lyons's office was mysteriously cut. "When I returned to the office that night at 12:30 A.M. with colleagues I found I couldn't turn on any of the lights," he said, in his statement to police. "It seemed as though we had suffered a power cut. But other offices in the same building, and in other buildings nearby, remained alight, and the street lights were working. I heard an indistinct noise, like ticking, and thought a bomb was on the premises, so I told everyone to get out and called the police."

Lyons told police he believed secret-service agents had broken into his office and either searched the premises or planted surveillance and listening devices there.

Just hours after they arrested seven paparazzi, the police and judiciary in Paris knew that these men would never be found guilty of causing Diana's death. Even though they would play out the charade and go on to arrest three other photographers who had leaped, like camera-toting ghouls, around the dying princess, the police were certain they could never be held responsible for the crash. The witnesses were adamant. Disgusting though their behavior had been, the paparazzi were just not there when the Mercedes hit the concrete pillar.

The word from above was still the same, though— and growing impatient. A quick and simple answer must be found. The unprecedented outpouring of public grief in England had taken the government and the royal family by surprise. No one had doubted Diana's popularity, but her death had tapped into a level of emotional reaction which transcended anything on record.

Whispers of assassins having been unleashed in Paris had already begun. No one wanted to believe that a simple traffic accident could rob them of the vibrant, passionate young woman—the People's Princess, as Tony Blair dubbed her in an emotional eulogy which reflected a nation's thinking.

If the assassination rumor took hold, or the official French inquiry became bogged down for any length of time with no official information being released, then there was no knowing how angry the masses might become or how they might react.

A well-founded police belief is that more than eighty percent of road traffic accidents are the fault of the driver. So in their search for a culprit, the French authorities automatically turned their attention to Henri Paul. French officials believed then, as they do now, that no one would ever know the real truth. There was enormous pressure on them all to wrap it up quickly and produce a verdict. That not everything was fully investigated, or is ever going to be fully investigated, was never of great concern to the Criminal Brigade. The obvious answer—that it was the driver's fault—appealed to everybody. It was such a natural explanation: obvious and therefore good.

First inquiries had revealed surprisingly mixed background information about the forty-one-year-old bachelor, some of it highly conflicting. On the one hand there emerged the profile of a quiet, almost shy, unassuming man, loyal to his tight-knit circle of close friends, who was a keen and competitive tennis player with an unusual hobby—flying light airplanes. As a boy he had won prizes for playing the violin and piano, and he had a passion for Liszt and Schubert. People saw him as a rather serious, slightly correct, though sociable type, and a modest drinker. Three of his closest friends swore they had never seen him the worse for wear through drink.

The more sinister side that emerged was of a professional seller of secrets, a man contracted to a host of intelligence-agency masters—at the right price. Among other secret services which employed him, Henri Paul was an agent for MI6. He had joined the Ritz Hotel in 1986, tipped off to the vacancy by a policeman friend, and was soon "helping" local police, French Intelligence and various foreign agencies with their inquiries. With the flow of business tycoons, film celebrities, foreign statesmen, arms dealers and international criminals through the hotel, a security executive was well placed to uncover much sought-after information about its clientele. As acting head of security he had a twenty-strong staff, and knew what was happening in every nook and cranny in the building.

To the French authorities, Henri Paul made an attractive villain. The police believed they could conceal some of the more unsavory aspects of his work for them and still present him as a suitably repulsive character who received large payments from selling the personal secrets of trusting guests like Princess Diana to the scavenging jackals of the international intelligence community. Add to this the emotive "facts" that he was a drunk alcoholic and driving at 120 miles per hour when the car crashed, and it could be guaranteed that little sympathy would flow in Paul's direction.

It is now accepted that the blood sample purporting to come from Henri Paul's body had not been analyzed by the time the statement came from the Criminal Brigade and the judiciary on September 1 that he had been three times over the French legal drink limit, with 1.75g of alcohol per liter of blood.

On September 1, Judge Hervé Stephan had still

not been appointed; neither had his assistant, Judge Marie-Christine Devidal. So just who did authorize the leak about the alcohol content of Paul's blood, and why? Under France's archaic secrecy laws, no announcement should have been made at that time. It is impossible to discover who was responsible for ordering the official leak. But the authorities, fronted by the Criminal Brigade, between them, had chosen a perfect fall guy, and wanted the public to know about him.

Henri Paul was "as drunk as a pig," said the leak, with the equivalent of two bottles of wine or a dozen whiskies having been guzzled that night, and careening madly along at 120 miles per hour when he lost control and rammed the concrete pillar in the Alma tunnel. This dramatic and evocative statement made headlines around the world which, according to a reliable police source in Paris, was the principal idea. "It certainly stopped people speculating about other reasons for the crash," he said, and when a second leak, eight days later, confirmed the alcohol levels and added that Paul had also taken Prozac, a prescription drug to shake off depression, and Tiapridal, a drug to cope with the side effects of alcoholism, the character assassination was complete.

"A frightening cocktail of drugs and booze," doctors were quoted as saying, "made him totally unfit to drive." The drugs, combined with the alcohol, would have caused him to act even more irresponsibly, it was claimed. That the traces of the two drugs found in the hair samples were too small to measure was conveniently omitted from the police leak. They were levels of someone taking medication—not an indication of drug abuse.

At that time police were maintaining the car was traveling at between 90 and 100 miles per hour when it crashed. But the Criminal Brigade knew that this information was untrue. They already knew the real speed of the Mercedes to have been sixty-four miles per hour when it crashed. That was the speed stamped on the speed-camera photograph taken only a couple of seconds before impact at the tunnel entrance. That picture of the Mercedes, time-stamped with the speed and date, was shown to French journalist Patrick Chauvel by a disgruntled traffic cop, whose department's investigation of the crash was summarily rejected by the Criminal Brigade. The photograph, a copy of which I have seen, was also in Judge Stephan's files.

Yet this was by no means the most blatant omission the Criminal Brigade deliberately made in its leaks. Nowhere was it mentioned that the blood tests on Henri Paul had revealed a major alien constituent in his blood which they should not have found there, and for which there is no acceptable explanation. Had an independent investigation, undertaken by the Ritz Hotel and handled by ex-Scotland Yard detective chief superintendent John McNamara, not obtained copies of the original pathology reports, it is certain the police would never have revealed these vitally important, and from their point of view extremely embarrassing, concealed facts; and it is equally unlikely that Judge Stephan would have included them in the truncated version of his report that was eventually published.

As it is, the facts did not come to light until June 1998—ten months after the crash and after Henri

Paul had been found guilty, worldwide, of having caused the death of Princess Diana.

The police had intended these hidden files to remain concealed forever. The shock revelation that they had been ferreted out was catastrophic news for the Criminal Brigade. The blood samples, allegedly coming from Henri Paul, contained massive levels in the one, and almost lethal levels in the second, of carbon monoxide—the kind of levels that are normally only found in a car-exhaust suicide victim. The attempts to explain the levels, 12 percent in the sample of blood from the femoral vein, and 20.7 percent from the heart, were scientifically and medically nonsensical.

The report by French pathologists on their autopsy on what was allegedly Henri Paul's body is hardly one which inspires confidence.

The time that the autopsy was carried out was not noted on the report; neither was the duration of the pathologists' investigation. There were also a number of obvious errors, including a statement in one part of the report that his cervical column was intact, whereas elsewhere it is described as being fractured. There is not even a description of how Henri Paul's body was identified as being his.

The pathologists concluded that during the few breaths he might possibly have taken immediately following the crash, he inhaled carbon monoxide which was leaking from the airbag. This was sufficient, they claimed, when taken in conjunction with carbon monoxide already in his blood from an allegedly high level of cigarette smoking, to produce similar levels of carbon monoxide to those which were found in his body.

The process of movement of carbon monoxide

and carboxyhemoglobin would be as follows. From the lung it travels to the left side of the heart, from where it is circulated through the body and then returns to the right side of the heart. This makes the assumption that such circulation as described above was in the process of taking place in the body of Henri Paul, producing a very high level of carbon monoxide in his heart and a high, albeit lower, level of carbon monoxide in his limbs.

Four incontrovertible facts make nonsense of this pathetic attempt by supposedly professional physicians to explain the inexplicable.

1. Mercedes-Benz states categorically that their airbags do not contain any carbon monoxide.
2. There was no other source of carbon monoxide in the Mercedes enabling Henri Paul to gasp in large amounts in his dying moments, as confirmed by the absence of carbon monoxide in the other victims' blood.
3. The French autopsy report states, as fact, that on impact, the thoracic aorta of Henri Paul was ruptured. "The flow of blood from the left side of the heart must have stopped at that moment," says a team of four renowned pathologists acting for Henri Paul's family.

Professors John Oliver and Peter Vanezis of the Department of Forensic Medicine at the University of Glasgow, and Professors P. Mangin and T. Krompecher of the Institut de Médecine Legale of the University of Lausanne, Switzerland, unanimously concluded that, "There could have been no passage of carbon monoxide from the left side of the heart to the rest of the body, and none could have returned to the right side of the heart. Accordingly, the high level of carbon monoxide in the sample of blood taken from the limb simply cannot be explained as resulting from inhalation of carbon monoxide from any source, and as the pathologists themselves appear to accept, cannot be explained merely by smoking.

"An even more fundamental issue is that since there could have been no passage of carboxyhemoglobin from the left to the right side of the heart, probably no more than in the range of 5 percent to 8 percent would be found in the blood of a heavy smoker.

"The pathologists' findings and conclusions on the issue, for reasons explained, are physically impossible and cannot be sustained."

4. Had Henri Paul had these levels of carbon monoxide in his blood at the time of the autopsy, it is estimated, using known rates of decrease in percentage per hour, then the level of carbon monoxide in his blood in the hour before the crash would have been at least thirty percent.

This is a near fatal level. Experts state that he would have been suffering from blinding headaches, probably vomiting and would have had great difficulty in walking properly. The brain, being deprived of oxygen, would not function correctly. Distance and time would be difficult to judge and he would lack coordination.

None of these symptoms are apparent from the mass of CCTV footage which covers his movements in the hour before the party left the hotel.

In short, this blood sample, which matched the alcohol content of the initial police leak, had a carbon monoxide content which proves it could not have come from Henri Paul. It is hardly surprising, therefore, that the French authorities have consistently refused to allow test specimens to be examined by outside pathologists, or that their top judge refuses to allow DNA samples from those specimens to be compared with DNA samples from Henri Paul. Astonishingly, Commander Mules still maintains the ridiculous fantasy that the carbon monoxide was inhaled during the last moments of Henri Paul's life. Mercedes airbags, according to the Paris Criminal Brigade, still contain large amounts of carbon monoxide—irrespective of the denials of the car's manufacturer.

Perhaps they would benefit from a chat with their own firemen. Those attending the crash were wearing carbon monoxide detectors. None of these indicated any trace of the gas in or near the wreckage.

What is beyond argument is that there were twenty-two other victims of "investigable death" in Paris that night. I was told by an extremely reliable police informant, attached to the city's pathology units, that one of the victims of "investigable death" that night was a man with money and marital problems, taking drugs for depression, who had drunk over half a bottle of vodka, before attaching a hose from the exhaust of his car to the interior and killing himself by sucking in carbon monoxide.

A sample of this man's blood would certainly have shown all the constituents of that purporting to come from Henri Paul, and would have had a similarly high percentage of carbon monoxide in it. Identifying the source of this carbon monoxide would have presented no problem. It would certainly have shown alcohol three times the legal limit, which was, for the police, the main criterion. The sky-high carbon monoxide content was clearly something which they had not anticipated—hence the bungled attempt at a cover-up.

My police informant refused to accept any payment for supplying the above information. He did so because he felt a major injustice had taken place and that Henri Paul had been made a scapegoat for something for which he was not responsible. He also pointed out that pathologists have been unable to explain the equally embarrassing autopsy report which showed that Henri Paul displayed absolutely no signs of the liver damage normally found in heavy drinkers, or even regular drinkers.

The police, not unexpectedly, utterly refuse to identify any of the other twenty-two persons classified as "investigable deaths" who were dealt with that night. Their pathology results are guarded more closely than the French mint.

Whether the switch was made accidentally or deliberately, I have no doubt at all that the blood samples purporting to have come from Henri Paul were not taken from the Ritz security chief's body, and were almost certainly from the body of an anonymous suicide victim.

Clearly Judge Hervé Stephan was not impressed with any of the answers given him by doctors.

"The blood is the great mystery of the affair," he concluded.

FIFTEEN

Renegade former MI6 agent D/813317 Richard John Charles Tomlinson, who worked for the British Secret Intelligence Service from September 1991 to April 1995, says he believes there are documents held by his former employers that would yield important evidence into the cause and circumstances leading to the death of Princess Diana and Dodi Fayed.

When Tomlinson was first recruited by MI6, he was expected to be a high-flyer. His qualifications were as good as they get. A British and New Zealand citizen, he was educated at Cambridge University and was later a Kennedy Memorial Scholar at the Massachusetts Institute of Technology. He is fluent in French, German and Spanish. He was recruited, under the trusted old-boy university network, as a fast-stream intelligence officer into Her Majesty's Secret Intelligence Service, MI6, in 1991, and completed the six-months initial training course with the highest marks ever achieved.

In revealing inside secrets on how Princess Diana died, Tomlinson lifted the lid on the murky world of MI6 and told how Diana was spied on for fifteen years until the night of the crash.

"I saw various documents during my four years with MI6 that I believe would provide new evidence and facts into the investigation of their deaths," he says. "I also heard various rumors which—though I was not able to see supporting documents—I am confident were based on solid fact."

Tomlinson, whose job also involved recruiting new spies for England, spoke out against some of the extreme methods being used by MI6 and was dismissed without warning and without reason in 1995. Intelligence chiefs kept their reasons hidden under the Official Secrets Act.

In 1996, under his campaign against MI6 abuses of power, Tomlinson wrote, but did not publish, a book. A five-page synopsis he gave to Australia's Transworld Publishers was handed to MI6 and Tomlinson was arrested under the Official Secrets Act. Writing from his prison cell while on remand, he said in the *Sunday Times* that he saw himself as a political prisoner, and described the extraordinary lengths MI6 had gone to hunt him down. He said he relished the opportunity from open court to expose the hypocrisy, dishonesty, unaccountability and mismanagement at MI6.

The opportunity was never granted. On December 18, 1997, Tomlinson was sentenced at the Old Bailey to twelve months in a maximum-security prison. In passing sentence, the judge said he was doing so "in the national interest."

It was after his release from prison that he began seriously probing the Alma tunnel death crash, and realized he recognized some of the personalities involved. "I do believe there was MI6 involvement in the crash which killed Princess Diana and the others," he says. "I came across Henri Paul's personal file in 1992 while I was involved in a complicated operation to smuggle advanced Soviet weaponry out of the Soviet Union. The operations involved a large cast of officers and agents of MI6. On more than one occasion, meetings between various figures in the operation took place at the Ritz Hotel in Paris. There were several intelligence reports of these meetings in the file written by a Paris-based MI6 officer, identified in the file by a coded designation.

"The source was an informant in the Ritz Hotel, who again was identified in the files by a code number. The MI6 officer paid the informant in cash for his information. I became curious, as his number cropped up several times and he seemed to have extremely good access to the goings-on in the Ritz Hotel, and I ordered his personal file from MI6's central file registry.

"I learned that the informant was a security officer at the Ritz Hotel. Intelligence services always target the security officers of important hotels because they have such good access to intelligence. I remember, however, being mildly surprised that the nationality of this informant was French, and this stuck in my memory because it is rare that MI6 succeeds in recruiting a French informer. This was Henri Paul.

"I am confident the relationship between him and MI6 would have continued until his death, because MI6 would never willingly relinquish control over such a well-placed informant. I am sure that the personal file of Henri Paul will therefore contain notes of meetings between him and his MI6 controling officer right up until the point of his death.

"I firmly believe that these files will contain evidence of crucial importance to the circumstances and causes of the incident that killed Monsieur Paul, together with the Princess of Wales and Dodi Fayed.

"The most senior undeclared officer in the local MI6 station would normally control an informant of Monsieur Paul's usefulness and seniority. In Paris, at the time of his death, there were two relatively experienced but undeclared MI6 officers. The first was Nicholas Langman. The second was Richard Spearman. I firmly believe that either one or both of these officers will be acquainted with Monsieur Paul, and most probably also met Monsieur Paul shortly before his death. I believe that either or both of these officers will have knowledge that will be of crucial importance in establishing the sequence of events leading up to the death of Princess Diana.

"Mr. Spearman in particular was an extremely well-connected and influential officer because he had been, prior to his appointment in Paris, the personal secretary to the chief of MI6, David Spedding. As such he would have been privy to even the most confidential of MI6 operations. I believe that there may well be significance in the fact that Richard Spearman was posted to Paris in the month immediately before the deaths.

"I told Judge Stephan that I believed MI6 might have ordered Henri Paul to drive into the tunnel. He would not have known it was an ambush."

Tomlinson said that it was also in 1992 that he saw a three-page document which was an outline plan to assassinate the Serbian leader, President Slobodan Milosevic. "The plan was fully typed and attached to a yellow 'minute' board, signifying that this was a formal and accountable document. It was entitled 'The need to assassinate President Milosevic of Serbia'.

"It was noted that the document had been circulated to several senior MI6 officers, including the head of Balkan operations and the personal secretary to the chief of MI6. The proposal was to cause Milosevic's car to crash in a tunnel using a brilliant flash of light at just the right moment to blind the driver. Some elements were chillingly similar to those involved in the death of Princess Diana."

During his service in MI6, Tomlinson also learned, unofficially and secondhand, something of the links between MI6 and the royal household.

"MI6 are frequently and routinely asked by the royal household, usually via the Foreign Office, to provide intelligence on potential threats to members of the royal family on overseas trips. This service would frequently extend to asking friendly intelligence services, such as the CIA, to place members of the royal family under discreet surveillance, ostensibly for their own protection.

"This was particularly the case for the Princess

of Wales, who often insisted on doing without overt personal protection, even on overseas trips. Although contact between MI6 and the royal household was officially only via the Foreign Office, I learned while in MI6 that there was unofficial direct contact between certain senior and influential MI6 officers and senior members of the royal household. There is an arrogant faction in MI6, a part of the Oxbridge clique, which doesn't try to hide dedication to the royal family and their self-appointment as defenders of the realm.

"I firmly believe that MI6 documents would yield substantial leads on the nature of their links with the royal household, and would yield vital information about MI6 surveillance on the princess in the days leading to her death."

Tomlinson gave much of this information to Judge Hervé Stephan on Friday, August 28, 1998—almost exactly one year after Diana's murder.

"The lengths MI6, the CIA and the DST took to deter me giving evidence, and subsequently stop me talking about it, strongly suggests they had something to hide," he says. "They have continued to attempt to harass me at every opportunity they can.

"On July 31, 1998, the DST arrested me in my Paris bedroom. Although I had no record of violent conduct, I was arrested with such ferocity, and at gunpoint, that I received a broken rib. I was taken to the headquarters of the DST and interrogated for thirty-eight hours. Despite my repeated requests, I was never given any justification for the arrest and was not shown the arrest warrant. Even though I was released without charge, the DST confiscated from me my laptop computer and

Psion organizer. They illegally gave these to MI6 who took them back to the U.K. They were not returned for six months.

"The following week, on Friday, August 7, 1998, I boarded a Qantas flight at Auckland, New Zealand, for a flight to Sydney, Australia, where I was due to give a television interview on Channel Nine.

"I was actually in my seat awaiting take-off when an official boarded the plane and told me to get off. It seemed the airline had received a fax 'from Canberra' saying there was a problem with my travel papers. When I asked to see the fax I was told it was not possible.

"I don't think the fax existed. The whole thing was just a ploy to keep me in New Zealand so the police there could take further action.

"Within half an hour of my returning to the hotel, both the police and the NZSIS, the New Zealand Secret Intelligence Service, raided me. After being detained and searched for about three hours, they eventually confiscated from me all my remaining computer equipment that the French DST had not succeeded in taking from me. Again, I didn't get some of those items back until six months later.

"Moreover, shortly after I had given my evidence to Judge Stephan, I was invited to talk about this evidence in a live television interview on America's NBC television channel. I flew from Geneva to JFK airport on Sunday, August 30, 1998, to give the interview in New York on the following Monday morning.

"Shortly after arrival at John F. Kennedy airport, the captain of the Swiss Air flight told all passengers to return to their seats. Four U.S. immigration authority officers entered the plane, came straight to my seat, asked for my passport as identity, and then frogmarched me off the plane. I was taken to the immigration detention center, photographed, fingerprinted, manacled by my ankle to a chair for seven hours, served with deportation papers, and then returned on the next available plane to Geneva.

"I was not allowed to make any telephone calls to the representatives of NBC awaiting me at the airport. The U.S. immigration officers, who were all openly sympathetic to my situation and apologized for treating me so badly, openly admitted they were acting under instructions from the CIA.

"In January the next year I booked a chalet in the village of Samoens in the French Alps for a ten-day snowboarding holiday with my parents. I picked them up with a rental car from Geneva airport on January 8 and set off for the French border.

"At the French customs post our car was stopped and I was detained. Four officers from the DST held me for four hours. At the end of this interview I was served with deportation papers and ordered to return to Switzerland.

"In the papers my supposed destination had been changed from Chamonix to Samoens. This was because when first questioned I told a junior DST officer my destination was Chamonix. When a senior officer arrived an hour or so later, he crossed out 'Chamonix' and inserted 'Samoens' without even asking or confirming this with me. I believe this was because MI6 had told them of my true destination, having learned the information through surveillance on my parents' telephone in the U.K.

"My banning from France was entirely illegal under European law. With a British passport I am entitled to travel freely within the European Union. MI6 did a deal with the DST to have me banned from France because they wanted to prevent me from giving further evidence to Judge Stephan's inquest, which at the time I was planning to do.

"Whatever MI6's role in the events leading to the death of the Princess of Wales, Dodi Fayed and Henri Paul, I am absolutely certain that there is substantial evidence in their files that would provide crucial evidence in establishing the exact causes of this tragedy.

"I believe they have gone to considerable lengths to obstruct the course of justice by interfering with my freedom of speech and travel, and this, in my view, confirms my belief that they have something to hide. I believe that the protection given to MI6 files under the Official Secrets Act should be set aside in the public interest in uncovering once and for all the truth behind these dramatic and historically momentous events.

"Why don't they yield up this information? They should not be allowed to use the Official Secrets Act to protect themselves from investigation into the deaths of three people."

SIXTEEN

During his service with MI6, Richard Tomlinson had discovered that one of the paparazzi photographers who routinely followed the Princess of Wales was a member of the UKN, a small corps of part-time British Secret Intelligence Service agents who provide miscellaneous services to MI6 such as surveillance and photographic expertise. This man was believed to be James Andanson who was, at the time of Diana's murder, under investigation by the French equivalent of Special Branch.

He was suspected of having had a hand in several killings, and was known to be working for at least one foreign intelligence agency. Tomlinson said, "Only an examination of UKN records would yield the identity of this photographer. But he is believed to be James Andanson."

One of his colleagues in the SIPA photo agency in Paris, for which he worked, confirmed that

Andanson had boasted of working for French and British Intelligence.

One French Special Branch source said in a video-recorded interview, "He boasted to friends and neighbors—people who were close to him—of having been in the tunnel and of photographing and even taping the last moments of Diana in the tunnel. I think that James Andanson did not work alone, and it's likely he was run by, or manipulated by one or more security services or a team, whose mission it was, at some point, to eliminate, harass or sometimes compromise a personality. Andanson was passing on information. People have talked of his links with British and French security services and that has never been proved. But it's a hypothesis that cannot be ruled out."

The widow of one of Andanson's friends said, "He told me he was in the tunnel but he wasn't caught by the police. He was too canny for that."

Was the photograph mentioned by the Special Branch agent—the one which Andanson boasted about—the very same photograph which is secretly contained in the judicial files in Paris. If so, and it is inconceivable that two such last-moment photographs of the Princess exist, then how did it come into police possession—and more importantly, why was it not mentioned by the judge in his report?

The answer can only be that it was part of a major cover-up to Diana's murder. Its discovery may also prove to be the answer as to why Andanson was killed four years ago. He talked too freely and too often, and because of it had to be silenced before revealing too much, one intelligence source advised me. "He was a danger and had to be got rid of."

Andanson was one of the top paparazzi in Europe, who had amassed a million-pound fortune taking pictures of celebrities and royalty. He flew the Union Jack over his house to show his love of Britain. On one occasion he made £100,000 on a single picture of Prince Charles kissing Tiggy Legge-Bourke, the former nanny to William and Harry, in Klosters, the Swiss ski resort.

He had photographed Diana throughout the summer, and French Special Branch, in an operation unconnected with her murder, secretly copied his private diaries, and learned that he had spent the day of August 23 actually on board the *Jonikal* at the same time as Diana and Dodi. The source explained, "It is not normal for a journalist like Andanson to be on board a yacht like that. But he was on the *Jonikal* for the whole day. His diary clearly shows the entry."

Jean-Claude Mules said he had learned that Andanson had made a deal with Diana in St. Tropez for pictures of her in a high-cut swimsuit. But there is no way of telling if the two items are connected.

Andanson had made a career of traveling around Europe photographing Princess Diana, yet he claimed not to have been in Paris to snap Diana on, possibly, one of the most important days of her life—her engagement to Dodi Fayed.

He was also a paparazzo with political connections at the highest levels. He was friendly enough with former prime minister Lionel Jospin to ride pillion with him on a motorcycle. Said Tomlinson, "MI6 has a whole cadre of people like Andanson who simultaneously do their own job—their own profession. They happen to have skills that can be used occasionally by MI6 on a contractual basis."

Two weeks after the crash, the Criminal Brigade finally admitted that traces of white paint in scratches found on the Mercedes indicated that a slight collision had taken place in the mouth of the Alma tunnel. The trace of color on the front right wing and on the body of the right wing mirror of the Mercedes both originated from the same vehicle—a Fiat Uno built in Italy in the period 1983 to 1987.

Red-and-white optical debris found in the tunnel entrance in the right-hand lane also came from a Fiat Uno, and was part of a rear light of a vehicle built in Italy between May 1983 and September 1989.

The *Institut de Recherche Criminelle de la Gendarmerie Nationale* (IRCGN) experts deduced that it was a collision "three quarters behind," and at the moment of contact the speed of the Mercedes was faster than that of the Fiat Uno.

Judge Stephan reported that the driver of the Fiat Uno had not been able to be identified, despite extremely long and detailed investigations which had been made by the inquiry team. This is complete nonsense. According to Commander Mules, his men didn't even bother to search the whole of Paris for the mystery Uno, let alone France.

Wrote Clive Goodman, who interviewed Mules in November 2003, "Instead they checked just two suburbs, known as departments, near the tunnel, before deciding to give up."

Commander Mules said, "We limited ourselves

to these departments. We took into account the fact that it was late and the driver must be going home, and witnesses said the car was registered in Paris. One cannot say that we did nothing." He scoffed at the idea of carrying out a nationwide search for the Uno. "It would be enormous to do that for the whole country. Think a little bit," he sneered.

There was never any suspicion that the driver just might have been an assassin and perhaps was not going home.

In February 1998, John McNamara and his team of investigators succeeded in doing what the Criminal Brigade had failed to accomplish. The white Fiat Uno had been sold to a dealer in October 1997, having undergone bodywork on the side and the rear light, and having been repainted.

The owner at the time of the crash was James Andanson.

The white paint found on the Mercedes matched that of the Uno. The Criminal Brigade waited two weeks to examine the car and interview Andanson. They claimed that when they saw the car it did not have tires or a battery. "It hadn't been used for months," said Commander Mules. This is just untrue. The car was with a dealer waiting to be sold. Andanson's colleagues insist he had been driving it frequently and recently.

"I was the one who questioned Andanson," said Mules. After what this Criminal Brigade commander had already admitted, this was not a statement to fill me with any degree of confidence. The photographer, it transpired, had handed Commander Mules a gas station receipt and a motorway toll ticket to prove that he had driven from his home in central France at 3:45 A.M. for a flight to Corsica from Orly airport. They were both receipts which could easily have been obtained for him by someone else. Nor did they prove that he had not been in the Alma tunnel at 12:25 A.M. Incredibly, they were enough to satisfy Commander Mules.

John McNamara vehemently disagrees with Mules's prognosis. "We have always maintained that Andanson was at the scene. That is a line of inquiry in which more investigation should have been done into his possible involvement."

Andanson's son, James, told police he thought his father was grape-harvesting in Bordeaux and had telephoned home that morning at about 4:30 A.M. Elizabeth Andanson gave a contrasting statement saying that she had been at home with her husband and he had left at 4 A.M. She explained these inconsistencies by saying that James, her husband, was always coming or going and it was difficult to recall his precise movements. "The family was very used to that and so never paid a great deal of attention to the times he came and went."

Confidential police forensic reports contained in Judge Stephan's report placed Andanson squarely at the center of events in the Alma tunnel. "They indicate that paintwork and plastics from a white Fiat Uno, owned by Andanson, match exactly evidence recovered from Diana's Mercedes, which clipped a Uno before crashing.

"The computive analysis of the infrared spectra characterizing the vehicle's original paint, reference Bianco 210, and the trace on the side-view mirror of the Mercedes, shows that their absorption bands are identical," says one report.

In layman's terms, the paint scratches from the

Fiat Uno found on the side-view mirror of the Mercedes were identical to the paint samples taken from the matching spot on Andanson's Fiat Uno.

But Commander Mules chose to turn Andanson loose.

Judge Stephan had concluded, totally illogically, that in any case the Fiat Uno played no more than a "passive" part in the tragedy. But a high-speed collision between the two cars, even if only glancing, and with the Mercedes swerving to avoid the slower car, could well have led to the eventual crash. The evidence from a reliable police witness of the Uno having been waiting for the Mercedes, and therefore having possibly deliberately tried to force it off course and off the road, was seemingly ignored by the judge.

Crash specialists Michel Nibodeau-Frindel and Bernard Amouroux, commissioned by Judge Stephan, reported, "The Mercedes was more likely to have gone off course as a result of trying to avoid hitting the Fiat, rather than being knocked off course by it." This is exactly the scenario that was intended.

If the presence of the Uno was entirely innocent, it is very odd that the driver, even anonymously, has not found a means of passing on his version of events, having had the best possible view of anyone. James Andanson may have denied to police that he was in Paris chasing Diana, but according to the widow of a neighbor he boasted openly of having not only been in Paris, but present at the moment Diana was killed. That could only have been at the wheel of his Fiat Uno.

* * *

So what was the truth about Andanson's undercover activities being probed by the French Special Branch?

It was French writer Dominica Labarrière who first became convinced that former prime minister Pierre Bérégovoy had not committed suicide in 1993, but had been assassinated. In his book *Cet homme a été assassiné*, Labarrière explained that Bérégovoy, a devoted family man, had left no word of goodbye. His notebook, which had been in his pocket half an hour before his death, had disappeared. It probably, he speculated, mentioned the identity of the last person he met.

The exit wound in his head was too small for that associated with a .357 Magnum, the alleged suicide weapon, and he claimed there had been no real investigation of the death. The suicide verdict was brought in, under political pressure, in fifteen minutes over allegations about interest-free loans to buy an apartment.

Labarrière wrote that many businesses feared the former prime minister, who was an honest man and could have testified in court in a number of criminal cases. He concludes, "I also discovered that James Andanson, the former photographer paparazzi, was in Nevers on the day of Bérégovoy's death. He knew Bérégovoy well, and I am astonished that his name does not appear. According to me, James Andanson could have played a role in the fatal appointment."

There had been other occasions when Andanson had been with the victim at around the time of a sudden death or alleged suicide, and he was actively under investigation by the French Special Branch at the time of Diana's death. It prompted the telling comment by one Special Branch source that "James Andanson had a strange intuition—the art of photographing people who then died suddenly."

When Andanson himself died suddenly, in a most horrific way, it led some to conclude that his connection with the death of Diana and others may well have caused his own.

Nearly three years after the Paris crash, Andanson's barely identifiable body was found in the burned-out wreckage of his car in woodland near Nant. This remote part of the plateau in central France is used as an army training area, and Andanson's body was discovered by commandos on military exercise. They found the car locked but with no sign of the key. It had been locked from the outside.

Andanson was so badly burned he could only be positively identified using his DNA.

The location was suspicious in itself. The car had traveled two miles up a potholed cart track, across empty countryside, bumped a further mile uphill across cow pastures, and then forced its way through dense forest to a clearing which few locals even knew existed.

The inquest judge declared that Andanson had committed suicide—400 miles from his luxurious farmhouse and without leaving a note. But she did say that if any further evidence or new information could be offered then she would be prepared to reopen the investigation into Andanson's death.

There had been a suggestion from one of his colleagues at the SIPA agency that Andanson had killed himself because of marital problems. But his wife Elizabeth completely dismissed this idea, and she and his son totally rejected the verdict of suicide. They were convinced James Andanson had been murdered and pressed French officials to keep a murder investigation running. Senior policemen, however, rejected the idea out of hand. They say the suggestion of it being murder is sheer fantasy. The favored police version is that he took his own life by dousing himself and the car with petrol, and then setting a light to it. No one has attempted to explain the missing key to the locked car.

At her house, Le Manoir de la Bergerie, Mrs. Andanson spoke of the last time her husband came home from Paris on May 4, 2000. "He left almost at once for another job. During our marriage I had become used to his dashing in and out without saying where he had been or where he was going. There were periods when we hardly saw each other. I assumed he had gone back to Paris, but a gendarme came the next day to say they thought James's body had been found inside a car in Nant.

"There had been nothing unusual about James before he left. Everything had seemed normal. He had been stressed for a while, but I had put that down to the normal pressure of being a journalist. I didn't know of any enemies, but in his line of work anything is possible."

One obvious possibility, and the version favored in the intelligence community, is that Andanson had been talking too much and someone had decided to silence him before he revealed further telltale details. Or had he threatened to come clean about what really happened that infamous night, and offered photographic evidence?

Andanson's friend François Dard said, "He told us that he was there. He was behind them. He was following behind. He saw the accident and all but he wasn't stopped by the police. He left. It is impossible that he committed suicide. We are convinced of it. To be burned alive in a car—we don't believe it at all."

Said ex-MI5 officer David Shayler, "The white Fiat was traced to James Andanson. Other paparazzi have reported his connections to MI6, which has a long record of using journalists and photographers as agents. When interviewed by police, Andanson claimed not to be in Paris that night. Yet forensics indicated that the Fiat had been in the tunnel and had been sold after the crash.

"It is far more likely that the crash was the work of MI6 agents—as opposed to serving officers. Known as 'surrogates' or 'cut-offs', they are otherwise unconnected to the service so MI6 can drop the operation should the agents be caught.

"As part of the recruitment, agents are asked if they are prepared to be 'ethically flexible'. If the answer is no, they are not recruited."

In Paris, even though the police there knew of the strong links between the paparazzo and Princess Diana, none thought it worthwhile mentioning Andanson's bizarre alleged suicide to Judge Stephan. None of these facts was taken into account in the official inquiry.

John McNamara said, "I am personally convinced he was killed to stop him talking about

Princess Diana's murder. He was a part-time intelligence agent, and therefore expendable. He had obviously become a liability and had to be got rid of."

As in the case of President Kennedy's assassination, could people close to the center of the investigation be targeted by the killers?

What happened in Paris the week after Andanson's death became public, did prompt the suggestion, in several quarters, that there might have been a threat to reveal photographic evidence which showed what happened on the night of the crash, and that this brought about his murder. In June 2000, an armed robbery took place at the SIPA photo agency where Andanson had worked. Three armed men, wearing balaclavas or ski masks, shot a security guard in the foot and held dozens of employees hostage for three hours. Despite phone calls from staff to the police, the Paris gendarmerie failed to respond, convincing observers that the raiders themselves were members of the French security service. "They seemed to know exactly what they were looking for and were confident enough to remain in a busy building for several hours, though they stole nothing of real value," said one SIPA employee.

The raiders dismantled all the security cameras in the offices and did not seem at all concerned about police rescuers arriving at the scene. Many of the staff believed the raid was related to Andanson's death, as the gang targeted specific offices where Andanson's royal pictures were stored. They removed cameras, laptop computers and computer hard drives where pictures were stored.

It was very reminiscent of the two raids mounted on the London photo agencies on the night after the crash.

Was there evidence of Andanson's presence in the tunnel? What, and whom did his photographs reveal that made a daylight raid by French secret service officers so imperative? It is now doubtful we will ever know. But if Diana's death was a simple accident why was this raid necessary at all?

Some of the answers about the Fiat Uno may have been revealed, but the whereabouts of the motorcycle and its driver and passenger remain a complete mystery.

The French inquiry seems to have made no attempt to track them down.

The importance of the motorcycle and its riders was highlighted by Anthony Scriver QC, a former chairman of the Bar Council, in an ITV documentary as long ago as September 1999, after the French inquiry findings were first published. He said that under French law "there is certainly enough evidence to charge that missing motorcyclist with manslaughter."

In his truncated final report Judge Stephan does not refer to the motorcycle at all, and in referring to the Fiat Uno, uses phrases such as "its role could only have been a passive one" and "contact only consisted of a simple scrape." He concludes that the Mercedes was rendered difficult to control "all the more so because of the presence of the Fiat Uno at the entrance to the tunnel."

SEVENTEEN

The blame may have been laid on the gravestone of Henri Paul, but there are those among the British Establishment who know the real truth. They are the same men who, when the public demanded a Westminster Abbey burial for Diana, found it "delightful" that she should be buried on an unknown island at the estate of her family's stately home. They hoped the public's memory of the princess would be allowed to fade quickly.

Fat chance. The public, cheated out of a place where she could be mourned by the nation and cheated out of a proper, official investigation into her death, deserve after all these years to be told, honestly, the real facts.

Like the assassination of President John F. Kennedy, everyone remembers where they were when they heard of the death of Princess Diana. While Britain wept, and bewildered Londoners gathered outside the black, iron railings at Buckingham

Palace, not everyone shared the same sense of grief. Among the highest echelons of the British Establishment, smiles were being exchanged at the news of the death of Diana. At last, they thought, the woman who had become a thorn in the side of the royal family would no longer plague them with her tantrums and indiscretions. No longer would the woman whose son would one day sit on the throne of England be photographed openly and wantonly kissing the Egyptian son of the owner of Harrods.

They were glad that the princess was dead. But these were the same people who had been too stupid to realize that, in life, Diana had been the jewel in the royal family's crown.

It was more than forty-eight hours before the royal family returned to London, bringing with them princes William and Harry. By then, the bewilderment of the people had turned to anger. They could not understand why this dysfunctional family had not returned to the capital where the Princess of Wales's body was lying in state. Or why, as they thronged the railings at Buckingham Palace, nobody was at home. Why was no flag flying at half staff? It was as if they had been abandoned; as if the royal family could not have cared less about the princess the public adored.

During those fateful hours, the royal family inflicted enormous damage upon itself from which it has never entirely recovered, because even the loyalist subjects of the Queen felt that, in some way they found hard to articulate, the memory of the princess had been betrayed. But there were some among the British Establishment who felt that it would be highly convenient if the public's memory of Princess Diana were allowed to fade as soon as possible.

While his mistress lay in the chapel at St. James's Palace, butler Paul Burrell, who had served Diana for ten years, was determined that he was going to preserve her memory—and the time bomb he knew she had left ticking away somewhere. The vultures had already begun to gather when Burrell, who was later charged with stealing 300 artifacts and bits and pieces belonging to Princess Diana, walked into her apartment at Kensington Palace to find her mother, Frances Shand-Kydd, rummaging through her belongings and shredding precious pieces of correspondence.

With her were Diana's sisters, Lady Jane Fellowes and Lady Sarah McCorquodale. Burrell and other Kensington Palace servants nicknamed Diana's sister Sarah "Mrs Crocodile." The women, according to Burrell, were systematically destroying all evidence of Diana's private life.

At Diana's funeral service, Earl Spencer, her foul-tempered, self-righteous brother, addressed the congregation, and tried to exorcise his guilt by verbally lashing the royal family for its indifference toward his sister. Sitting in near obscurity, in the "cheaper seats" at the Abbey, were Al Fayed and his beautiful, devoted, Finnish-born wife, Heini. Though they had lost their son, the Al Fayeds' presence was studiously ignored by the great and the good. There were no kind words of condolence for them. No arms placed sympathetically around their shoulders. They might as well have not existed. As they listened to the cant and the hypocrisy from Earl Spencer and then from that thwarted thespian Tony Blair, Mohamed Al Fayed whispered to his wife, "I'll get the murdering bastards. Whoever they are, I'll get them."

The Al Fayeds knew that Diana detested her brother and disliked her mother. She had not been on friendly terms with Earl Spencer since the time he had flatly refused her anguished pleas to allow her to have a small house in the grounds of Althorp. They also knew, because over dinner one night Princess Diana had told them, that she had not spoken to her mother since receiving a telephone call in which Frances Shand-Kydd had berated her daughter, telling her that she must "stop going out with fucking niggers." Burrell also knew of the family feuds, and of the cruel lack of support from her mother, her sisters and her brother after her failed marriage to Prince Charles.

Millions of people lined the streets of London to say their own goodbyes; ordinary, decent people who believed she should have been buried in Westminster Abbey. But again this would not have suited the Establishment. They feared that her tomb would become a point of pilgrimage for the millions who had loved and admired her. And that was the last thing they needed. So none of them objected when they discovered that immediately after the service in the Abbey, Earl Spencer intended to hijack the body of his sister and bury her in a lonely, sodden grave in the middle of an island in a little lake on the Spencer estate.

Though many people were puzzled and dismayed, not one member of the royal family raised a finger in objection. For them it meant that if Diana's tomb was out of sight, the public's memory of her would dim all the faster.

And there she lies, with the swans for company,

except for certain days a year when her greedy brother throws open the double iron gates of the estate and the public pour through to get a glimpse of the princess's grave from the lakeside— for a £10 a head admittance fee. The hypocrisy is that after so churlishly refusing his sister sanctuary on the family estate when she was alive, he now encourages the masses and the press to flood through the gates of his home to view the site of her grave. Outside interference in his family home no longer seems an issue.

He has also converted a few rooms in his stately pile into a museum to the memory of Diana. Since her death, the sister he betrayed in life has become a money raiser for the earl, which is why, I believe, he appeared so desperate to get his hands on the artifacts Paul Burrell claimed to have taken "for safe keeping."

POSTSCRIPT

The examining judge's report, in the end, ran to 7,000 pages, but only a truncated, 70-page version has ever been released by the French government. Hopefully, now that the British royal coroner has asked the Metropolitan Police to investigate Diana's death, they will be given the opportunity to examine the entire report in detail. It is well known that there was relentless political pressure for the judge to shut down his inquiry before it had pursued all the leads which it might have explored. It is to be hoped that similar pressure is not exerted on the British police or coroner.

Even the truncated version of Judge Stephan's report raised more questions than it was capable of answering, and this, more than anything else, is responsible for the great majority of people believing that her death was no accident.

One of the world's leading crime writers, Patricia

Cornwell, recently spent six months in England and France investigating the Alma tunnel crash on behalf of America's ABC television. Her intention had been to put together a program on what she believed to be an accident. Her conclusion echoes that of many other investigative writers and journalists. "The more I look into it, the more I have to say that I, personally, cannot dismiss the possibility of premeditated homicide," she said.

Personally, following my own two-year investigation, I am utterly convinced that Diana, Princess of Wales was murdered, and equally confident that the evidence to prove it lies in the files of the British Secret Intelligence Service and the CIA.

In 2003, Lord Hutton's inquiry into the death of weapons expert Dr. David Kelly managed to extract some answers from intelligence-agency records. Now the government should go a step further and order the intelligence service to make itself fully accountable. The complete archives should be opened up and made available to the Scotland Yard team appointed to probe Diana's death.

Anyone who looks at the facts of Diana's death, even stripped down to their bare essentials, cannot emerge without at least a suspicion that she was murdered. More than eighty-five-percent of British people believe that she was. The British authorities owe it to them and to Princess Diana herself to provide all of the evidence, and for once dispense with the Official Secrets Act. Otherwise this inquiry will be as much a cover-up as the one in France, and just as ineffectual.

* * *

In June 2004, as this book was undergoing its final edit, it was announced that the Archbishop of Canterbury, Dr. Rowan Williams, had dropped his objections to a marriage between Prince Charles and Camilla Parker Bowles. He had cleared the way for them to marry, it was said, after secret talks with the prince the previous year.

This followed a statement from his equally forgiving predecessor, former Archbishop of Canterbury, Lord Carey of Clifton, that by an amazing coincidence he too now felt it was natural that the couple should marry.

This must have come as devastating news for all of Diana's tens of millions of admirers and supporters worldwide.

I fully believe, as I have stated in this book, that one of the main contributory reasons for Diana's murder was to clear the way for Charles and Camilla to marry. It would seem after the years of purgatory to which this pair subjected the princess that they can ultimately anticipate not punishment for their wickedness, but the reward of a church wedding—together with the Church's blessing.

Should they really be allowed to benefit from their appalling deceit and betrayal? Should crime, if you're a royal, be allowed to pay? One can only hope not, and that the Queen, with whom the final decision rests, shows more moral courage than her toadying church leaders, and, as a powerful example to her people, forbids the marriage from ever taking place.

The People's Princess seems just as much in need of a champion in death as she ever did when she was alive. What better way could there be of showing the real depth of her admiration for her late daughter-in-law than for Queen Elizabeth to take up the gauntlet, as champion to the Princess, and do the right thing by Diana?

BIBLIOGRAPHY

Benson, Ross. *Charles, The Untold Story*. New York: St. Martin's Press, 1994.

Berry, Wendy. *The Housekeeper's Diary: Charles and Diana Before the Breakup*. New York: Barricade Books, 1995.

Blundell, Nigel. *Windsor versus Windsor*. London: Blake Publishing, Ltd., 1995.

Burrell, Paul. *A Royal Duty*. New York: Putnam Publishing Group, 2003.

Buskin, Richard. *Princess Diana: The Real Story*. New York: New American Library, 1992.

Campbell, Beatrix. *Diana, Princess of Wales: How Sexual Politics Shook the Monarchy*. London: The Women's Press, 1998.

Davies, Nicholas. *Diana: A Princess and Her Troubled Marriage*. Secaucus, NJ: Carol Publishing Group, 1992.

——— *Diana: Secrets and Lies*. London: AMI Books, 2003.

Delano, Julia. *Diana, Princess of Wales*. London: Smithmark Publishers, 1993.

Dimbleby, Jonathan. *The Prince of Wales: A Biography*. New York: HarperCollins, 1994.

Donnelly, Peter. *Diana—A Tribute to the People's Princess*. UK: Courage Books, 1997.

Fisher, Graham and Heather Fisher. *Charles and Diana: Their Married Life*. London: Hale, 1984.

Graham, Caroline. *Camilla: The King's Mistress*. London: Blake Publishing, Ltd., 1994.

Gregory, Martyn. *Diana: The Last Days*. London: Virgin Books, 2000.

Hewitt, James. *Love and War*. London: Blake Publishing, Ltd., 1999.

Hoey, Brian. *Charles and Diana: The 10th Anniversary*. New York: Penguin USA, 1991.

———— *Prince William*. Gloucestershire, UK: Sutton Publishing, 2003.

Hounam, Peter and Derek Mc Adam. *Who Killed Diana?* Berkeley, CA: Publishers Group West, 1998.

Jephson, P.D. *Shadows of a Princess*. New York: HarperCollins, 2000.

Kelley, Kitty. *The Royals*. New York: Little, Brown, and Co., 1997.

King, Jon and John Beveridge. *Princess Diana: The Hidden Evidence*. Devon, UK: Roundhouse Publishing, 2002.

Krohn, Katherine E. *Princess Diana*. UK: Lerner Publications, 1999.

Lefcourt, Peter. *Di and I*. New York: Random House, 1994.

Moore, Sally. *The Definitive Diana*. New York: McGraw-Hill, 1991.

Morton, Andrew. *Diana—Her New Life*. New York: Simon & Schuster, 1994.

——— *Diana—Her True Story*. New York: Simon & Schuster, 1992.

Pasternak, Anna. *Princess in Love*. New York: Penguin USA, 1994.

Rees-Jones, Trevor. *The Bodyguard's Story: Diana, the Crash, and the Sole Survivor*. New York: Warner Books, 2000.

Seward, Ingrid. *William & Harry: A Portrait of Two Princes*. New York: Arcade Publishing, 2003.

——— *The Queen and Di*. London: HarperCollins, 2000.

Snell, Kate. *Diana—Her Last Love*. London: Andre Deutsch, Ltd., 2000.

Vickers, Hugo. *Diana Remembered 1961–1997*. UK: Macmillan, 1997.

Wharfe, Ken. *Diana—Closely Guarded Secret*. Kansas City, MO: Andrews McMeel, 2002.

Wilson, Christopher. *The Windsor Knot*. New York: Citadel Press, 2002.

——— *A Greater Love: Prince Charles's Twenty-Year Affair with Camilla Parker Bowles*. New York: HarperCollins, 1994.

INDEX

Airbags, 192, 241, 242, 244

Aitken, Jonathan, 136–37

Al Fayed, Mohamed. *See* Fayed, Mohamed Al

Alma Tunnel, 11–12, 188–214, 224–26

Althorp, 29, 88, 107, 130, 272–73

Amouroux, Bernard, 262

Andanson, Elizabeth, 261, 265

Andanson, James, 13, 187–88, 193, 256–68

Andanson, James, Jr., 261

Anderson, Brian, 199

Anderson, Mabel, 52

Andrew, Duke of York, 72, 103–4

Angola, 127–29

Anne, Duchess of Westminster, 103

Anne, Princess, 21, 57, 61–70

Ardent, 159–60

Arlberg Hotel, 87

Arms trade, 16–17, 129, 134, 143–44, 162–63

Arnol, Serge, 203–4, 205, 210

Arsène Houssaye, rue, 187, 221–22

Arsov, Nikola, 210

Ascot, 111

Assassination, 7, 14–16, 15–16, 164–65, 192–93, 236–37, 251

Austin, George, Archdeacon of York, 110

Australia, 40, 41, 112–14, 253

Autopsies, 226–29, 232–33, 240–45

Aylard, Richard, 126

Bagehot, Walter, 91

Balmoral Castle, 36, 48, 73, 76–77, 222–23, 232–33, 270

Banamou, Serge, 203

Barrow Green Court, 222

Bashir, Martin, 46, 118–19

BBC, 118–19, 120

Bérégovoy, Pierre, 188, 263–64

Berry, James, 75

Berry, Wendy, 54, 77–78, 91, 100, 145

Birkhall, 83, 116

Blair, Tony, 18, 236, 271–72

Blood tests, 9–11, 228, 238–46

Bodyguards, 15, 150–51, 167, 169–70, 179

Bolehyde Manor, 22, 36–37, 65

Bolland, Mark, 126

Bonsor, Nicholas, 128–29

Bosnia, 128, 142–44, 208

Boyer, Philippe, 210–12
Britannia, 36, 47, 140
British Embassy, 150, 221, 223–24
British intelligence. *See* M15; M16
Brompton Hospital, 124–25
Bryer, Tania, 140–41
Buckingham Palace, 42, 44–45, 157, 160, 161, 222, 269–70
Bulimia, 42, 47, 48, 52, 56, 73
Burgess, Michael, 233
Burrell, Paul, 15, 84–85, 145–46, 232–33, 271, 272, 273
Burton, John, 233
Butt, Mark, 205

Cambodia, 113, 128
Cambon, rue, 181–84, 185
Camillagate, 102–6
Cannes, 59, 135
Carbon monoxide, 9–11, 241–44
Cardiac arrest, 211–12, 215, 216, 217–18
Carey, Lord, Archbishop of Canterbury, 45, 47, 120, 276
Carling, Julia and Will, 118, 122
Cellnet, 96
Central Intelligence Agency (CIA), 17, 157, 161–65, 251, 252, 253–54
Champs Elysées, 185–87
Chapman, Dr., 228–29, 233
Channel Nine, 253
Charles, Prince of Wales
  after death of Diana, 222–23, 231–33
  bedroom skills of, 23–24
  Camilla and, before marriage, 20–26, 37–39, 41–43; during marriage, 50, 52–53, 55, 72–77, 82–83, 87, 92–93, 102–6, 114–16; taped phone call, 102–6; wedding night, 44–45, 72–73
  courtship, 25–26, 35–39
  divorce, 46–47, 105, 110–11, 119–22, 126, 130, 158, 276–77
  Earl Spencer and, 88–89

  fights, 51–52, 54–55, 73–75, 91–92, 100
  as heir to throne, 109–11, 126
  honeymoon, 47–48
  jealousy of, 71–72, 76–77, 84
  Mannakee and, 58, 59, 60, 61
  Pink Mafia and, 30–31, 53–54
  polo accident, 75, 76, 77
  Prince Edward and, 159–61
  proposal, 39–40
  public life, 86, 87–88, 112–15
  Squidgy Tape and, 97–98
  as threat to Diana, 14–15
Chauvel, Patrick, 240
Cherruault, Lionel, 234–35
Chevènement, Jean-Pierre, 209, 217
Chez Armand, 177
Chez Benoit, 169, 172
Chopp, Nicola, 59–60
Church of England, 110–11, 126, 157–58, 276–77
Cirencester Polo Club, 25
Clarence House, 41
Clinton, Bill, 16–17, 128, 143–44, 162–63
Clinton, Hillary, 128, 144
Clochard-Bossuet, Father, 217–18
Conspiracy theories, 9–14, 215–16, 225, 236–37, 257–58
Cornwell, Patricia, 274–75
Coujard, Maude, 208–10
Cours Albert Ier, 188, 197
Cours la Reine, 186–87
Courtship, 25–26, 35–39
Criminal Brigade, 7–11, 197–214, 225–26, 237–46, 259–62
Cross, Peter, 57, 67–68
"Crown Jewels," 29, 85, 273
Cujo, 135, 139

Daily Express, 24
Daily Mail, 157, 168–69, 228–29
Daily Mirror, 38, 55–56, 136, 141
Daily Telegraph, 230
Dalby, Damien, 204–5
Daloman, Maniel, 217–18
Dard, François, 266
Darmon, Stéphane, 202, 210
Davies, Steve, 118

Dean, Gary, 201
Death certificate, 156
Delorme, René, 146, 147
Devidal, Marie-Christine, 239
Diana: Her True Story (Morton), 90–91
Dianamania, 49, 76–77, 111–13
Dickey, Christopher, 225
Dimbleby, Jonathan, 114–15
Direction de la Surveillance du Territoire (DST), 157, 252–53, 254–55
Divorce, 46–47, 105, 110–11, 119–22, 158
Dorzee, Sebastian, 205–6
Dourneau, Philippe, 166, 167, 169–70, 180–81, 221–22
Dunne, Philip, 72–73
Durrieux, Jean, 213
Dyrfed, Wales, 73

ECHELON project, 95–96
Edward VIII, 21–22, 117, 120, 167, 231
Edward, Earl of Wessex, 155–56, 159–61
Edwards, Bob, 38–39
Egypt, 89–90
Elizabeth, Queen Mother, 41, 51, 83, 111
Elizabeth II
    after death of Diana, 222–23, 270–71
    Diana's upstaging of, 56, 111–12
    divorce of Charles and Diana, 120–21
    on formal separation, 92
    Princess Anne and, 64, 67, 69
    Prince William and, 122–23
Elliott, Annabel, 73–74
Embalming, 28–29, 156, 226–29, 233
Emergency response, 202–8, 210–12, 215–20
Emergency room (ER), 217–19
Engagement, to Prince Charles, 40–45
Engagement ring, of Dodi Fayed, 147–50

Establishment, the, 136–37, 155–56, 158–59, 231, 269–73
Estonia, 229–30
Etoile Limousines, 180–81, 182
EuroBusiness, 230–31
Eyewitnesses, to accident, 197–202

Fayed, Dodi, 132–51, 155–95
    the accident and, 185–95
    after the accident, 221–24
    marriage plans, 27, 147–50, 178, 181–82
    Mediterranean cruises, 132–49
Fayed, Mohamed Al, 132–38, 142, 167, 178, 181–82, 221–24, 269, 271–73
Fayed, Samira Khashoggi ("Heini"), 134–35, 137, 147, 271–72
Federal Bureau of Investigation (FBI), 17
Fellowes, Lady Jane, 35–36, 44, 130–31, 231–33, 271
Fellowes, Sir Robert, 121
Fendel, François, 174, 175
Ferguson, Sarah, 72
Fermoy, Lady, 37
Fiat Uno, 12–13, 187–90, 192, 194–95, 200–202, 259–68
Fights and arguments, 51–52, 54–55, 73–75, 91–92, 100
Fisher, Kelly, 135, 139
Foreign Office, 251–52
Forge, Armand, 211–12
Fox, Uffa, 24
Fraser, Jason, 148
French Diplomatic Protection Squad, 150–51
French inquiry. *See* Criminal Brigade
French Intelligence, 8
French secret service (DST), 157, 252–53, 254–55
FSB, Andanson and, 256, 263–68
Funeral service, 269, 271–73

Gagliardone, Lino, 205–8
Garric, Claude, 176–77
Gatcombe Estate, 68

George VI, 21
Gibson, Wilfred, 67–68
Gilby, James, 93–98
Goldsmith, James, 73–74
Goldstein, Patrick, 219
Goodman, Clive, 115–16, 162,
   259–60
Gooroovadoo, Clifford, 207
Gourmelon, Xavier, 207–8,
   210–12
Great Ormond Street Children's
   Hospital, 82
Greece, 146–47, 229
Guards Club, 133
Gulf War, 84, 98
Gulf War Syndrome, 162–63
Guy's Hospital, 73

Hamilton, Neil, 136–37
Hammersmith and Fulham
   Mortuary, 228, 233
Handley-Greaves, Paul, 222
Hanger, Joan, 144
Harbour Club, 118
Harrods, 27, 133, 139, 149, 223
Harry, Prince of Wales, 28, 53,
   63, 71, 80, 81–82, 83–84, 87,
   100, 133, 270
Hermitage Hotel, 147–48
Hewitt, James, 29, 31, 60–61, 78–
   80, 98
Highgrove, 37, 52–55, 75–76, 81,
   91, 126, 130
Hoare, Diane, 108–9
Hoare, Oliver, 98, 108–9
Homosexuality, 30–31, 53–54
Honeymoon, 47–48
Hot Chocolate, 44
Household Cavalry, 52–53
Howe, Lord, 144
HRH, removal of title, 15, 121–
   22, 130
Hungary, 111–12

Imperial Suite (Ritz Hotel), 168–
   69, 173–74, 178, 179, 180–82
India, 85–87
Ingram, Sue, 88
Institut de Recherche Criminelle de
   la Gendarmerie Nationale
   (IRGGN), 259
Investigations, 7–14, 165, 196–
   214, 274–75
   blood tests and, 9–11, 228,
      238–46
   Coujard and, 208–10
   eyewitnesses and, 197–202
   Fiat Uno and, 12–13, 259–
      62
   Henri Paul and, 7–11, 161–62,
      237–46
   paparazzi and, 196–97, 202–8,
      210, 212–14
Islam, 155–58

Jacques, Andrew, 75
Jahan, Shah, 86
Jay, Marc Le, 212
Jay, Michael, 156, 209, 217, 218,
   220, 226, 232
Jephson, Patrick, 49, 54, 60
John, Elton, 43
Johnson, Lyndon B., 16
Jonikal, 132–33, 135, 140–41,
   147–48, 258
Jospin, Lionel, 258–59
Journal de Dimanche, 201

Kang, David, 113–14
Kelly, David, 275
Kelly, Kitty, 54–55
Kennedy, Jacqueline, 142
Kennedy, John F., 16, 267, 269
Kennedy Airport, 253–54
Kensington Palace, 65, 82–83,
   139–40, 144, 145, 271
Kensit, Patsy, 134
Keppel, Alice, 21–22
Khan, Hasnat, 122, 124–25,
   129–30
Khan, Nahid, 125
Khashoggi, Adnan, 134
Khashoggi, Samira. See Fayed,
   Samira Khashoggi
Kiernan, Ian, 113
Klosters, 72, 258
Knatchbull, Leonora, 82–83
Krompecher, T., 242–43

Labarrière, Dominica, 263–64
Land mines, 16–17, 126–29,
    142–44, 162–63
Langevin, Jacques, 210
Langman, Nicholas, 250
Last rites, 217–18
Latsis, John, 92
Laub, Steven, 178
Lawrence, Timothy, 68–69
Laurent, David, 200
Lavani, Gulu, 129–30
Lawson, Dominic, 229–31
Lawson, Nigella, 229
Lech, 83–84, 87
Lecomte, Dominique, 227, 233
Lee, Eric, 199–200
Legal drinking limit, 7, 9–10,
    241–44
Legge-Bourke, Tiggy, 258
Levistre, François, 198–99
Levistre, Valerie, 198–99
Lienhart, Andre, 227, 233
Life Guards, 78, 79
Linley, David, 30, 83–85
Lipsedge, Maurice, 73
London Geographical Society,
    129
Lotus, 95–96
Louise de Waldner, Baroness, 77
Lucard, Frederic, 182, 183
Lyons, Darryn Paul, 235–36

M15, 58, 96–97, 104
M16, 96–97, 156–58, 161–65,
    174, 179–80, 229–31,
    247–55, 266–67
McCorquodale, Sarah, 29, 35–
    36, 44, 131, 231–33, 271
McGrady, Darren, 146
McNamara, John, 172, 240, 260,
    261, 266–67
Mailliez, Frédéric, 204–8, 210–12
Major, John, 18, 93, 100, 104,
    127, 134
Mangin, P., 242–43
Mannakee, Barry, 56–61
Margaret, Princess, 38, 56, 85
Martinez, Christian, 203, 207,
    208, 210

Martino, Jean-Marc, 211–12,
    216–17
Massebeuf, Michel, 211–12,
    216–17
Massoni, Philippe, 209, 217
Melo, Dominique, 166–67
Mercedes Benz, 11, 166–67, 169–
    74, 181–202, 221–22, 226,
    242
Middlewick House, 53
Milosevic, Slobodan, 164, 251
Mistresses, royal men and, 83
Mobile phones, 171–72, 198,
    201, 204
Mobile surgery unit, 211–12,
    215–17
Monaco, 147–48
Monckton, Anthony Leopold
    Colyer, 229–31
Monckton, Rosa, 123, 146, 229–31
Monte Carlo, 147–48
Montefiore, Hugh, 111
Monteil, Martine, 8–9, 12–13,
    208–10, 225–26
Morgan, Piers, 141
Morton, Andrew, 48, 57, 90–91
Motorcycle, 189–92, 198–202, 268
Motorcycle outriders, for secu-
    rity, 150–51
Mountbatten of Burma, Lord
    Louis, 53
Mules, Jean-Claude, 8, 12–13,
    28–29, 156, 162, 197–98,
    202, 208–10, 227, 244,
    258–62
Musa, Jean-Francis, 221–22
Muslims (Islam), 155–58

National Security Agency
    (NSA), 17, 19, 95–96
NBC, 253–54
News of the World, 115–16, 162
Newsweek, 225
New York Daily News, 18
New York Times, 120
New Zealand Secret Intelligence
    Service (NZSIS), 253
Nibodeau-Frindel, Michel, 262
Nobel Peace Prize, 163
Northolt Airport, 87–88, 232

Obukhov, Pluton, 229–30
Odekerken, David, 203
Official Secrets Act, 161, 248, 255, 275
Old Bailey, 248–49
Oliver, John, 242–43
Onassis, Aristotle, 142
Onassis, Jacqueline Kennedy, 142
Ormley Lodge, 73–74
Oslo Conference, 17, 128

Pakistan, 124, 125, 129–30
Palmer-Tompkinson, Patsy, 76–77
Panorama, 46, 118–19, 120, 121
Paparazzi
    after the accident, 202–8, 220–21
    before the accident, 167, 168, 172–74, 185–95
    burglaries of, 234–36, 267–68
    cruises and, 137–38, 140, 141, 142, 147, 148
    scapegoating of, 196–97, 209–10, 212–14, 236–37
    security issues and, 150–51
Paranoia of Diana, 7, 14–16, 106–7, 119–20, 136–37
Paris Match, 213
Parker Bowles, Andrew, 20–23, 25, 36–37, 52–53, 61–67, 115–16
Parker Bowles, Camilla
    divorce from Andrew, 115–16
    Prince Charles and. See Charles, Prince of Wales, Camilla and
    Princess Diana and, 35–38, 44, 48, 73–75, 158
Parker Bowles, Thomas, 22
Park Lane, 139–40
Parry, Vivienne, 123–24
Paul, Henri, 149, 166–95
    background of, 161–62, 237–38
    scapegoating of, 7–11, 237–46, 269
Pavie, Alain, 218–19
Peat, Stephen, 59
Pennequin, Sébastien, 204–5
Pentagon, 16, 143–44, 162

Pètel, Eric, 9, 197–98, 203, 206–7, 212–14
Philip, Prince, 27, 36, 39, 48, 83, 90–91, 164–65, 222–23
Phillips, Mark, 21, 57, 63–70
Phillips, Zara, 64, 65
Pink Mafia, 30–31, 53–54
Pitié-Salpêtrère Hospital, 212, 216–20, 224, 231–32
Planet Hollywood, 111
Posner, Gerald, 176
Postmortem. See Autopsies
Postnatal (postpartum) depression, 52
Pravda, 229–30
Pregnancies, 50–51, 53
    alleged, 71, 156, 169, 220, 226–29, 231
Press Complaints Committee, 126
Prince of Wales, The: A Biography (Dimbleby), 115
Priory, The, 29
Private Eye, 23
Prozac, 239

Queen of Hearts campaign, 127–29, 142–44, 162–63

Range Rover, 166, 168, 172, 183–84, 221–22
Rat, Romuald, 202–3, 207, 210
Reagan, Nancy, 44
Reagan, Ronald, 95, 219–20
Red Cross, 128
Reeman, Cyril, 93, 95–96
Rees, Jeffrey, 233
Rees-Jones, Trevor, 15, 147, 148, 167, 169–70, 172–73, 177, 179–80, 182–84, 187–90, 192, 193, 204, 207–8, 221–22, 224
Reid, Sue, 228–29
Repossi, Alberto, 147–48, 149
Rescue operation. See Emergency response
Resuscitation attempts, 217–19
Richard III, 26
Rimington, Stella, 104

Riou, Bruno, 217–19
Ritz Hotel, 38, 139, 149–50, 161, 166–95, 223, 232, 238, 249
Roberts, Tanya, 134
Rochet, Thierry, 178–79, 184
Rogers, Rita, 146
Romsey, Lord, 44, 82–83
Roulet, Claude, 168, 169, 172, 181, 184, 223
Royal Ascot, 111
Royal Opera House, 82
Royal Protection Squad, 56–60, 67, 109

St. Andrew's University, 159–60
St. James's Palace, 28, 111, 123, 157, 161, 233
St. Tropez, 132–33, 135–38, 147, 258
St. Valentine's Day, 86–87
Sandhurst, 134
Sandringham, 39, 51
Sardinia, 140, 148–49
Scotland Yard, 275
Scriver, Anthony, 268
Seat belts, 167, 190, 192
Secret Intelligence Service (SIS), 93–98, 247, 275. See also M15; M16
Separation, 73, 92, 100–101, 104–5, 110–11
Serbia, 164, 251
Service d'Aide Médicale Urgente (SAMU), 210–12, 215–20
Seward, Ingrid, 123, 159, 160
Shand-Kydd, Frances, 20, 84, 130–31, 271–72
Shayler, David, 157, 192–93, 266
Shea, Michael, 38
Shields, Brooke, 134
Simpson, Wallis, 120, 167
Sinatra, Tony, 134
Sipa Pictures, 256–57, 264–65, 267–68
Skiing, 83–84, 87, 258
Smith, George, 29–31
Soames, Nicholas, 119–20
Sola, Laurent, 220–21, 235

SOS Médécin, 204
South Korea, 99–100
Soviet Union, 249
Spearman, Richard, 250–51
Special Branch, 58
Specialist heart surgeon, 217, 218
Spectator, 229–31
Spedding, David, 250–51
Speed camera, 11–12, 188, 189, 240
Speed limit, 188, 192, 194, 238, 240
Spencer, Charles, 20, 88–89, 107–8, 119–20, 130, 271–73
Spencer, John, 20, 43–44, 85–86, 87–89, 130, 133
Spencer, Raine, 88, 89, 133, 138, 142
Spencer, Victoria, 108
Spiritual advisers, 144, 146
Squidgy Tape, 93–98, 103
State Department, U.S., 18
Staverton, 38
Stephan, Hervé, 9, 157, 161–62, 187, 209, 226, 227, 233, 238–39, 246, 251, 252, 259, 261, 262, 266, 268, 274–75
Stephanie, Princess of Monaco, 134
Stromach, Ken, 55, 115–16, 117–18
Suicide attempts, 51–52
Sun, 93–98, 103
Sunday Mirror, 37–39, 164–65
Sunday People, 178, 198–99
Sunday Telegraph, 230
Sunday Times, 248
Sûreté, la, 8
Surveillance activity, 17–19, 29–31, 58–59, 60, 93–97, 102–5, 256–57
Swiss Air, 253–54

Taj Mahal, 86
Tawbase, Jane, 230–31
Tendil, François, 184
Teresa, Mother, 232
Tevere, Luigi del, 147
Thompson, Robert, 228

Tiapridal, 239
Tomlinson, Richard, 156–57,
        161, 164, 174, 175–76, 186,
        188, 190, 192, 229–31,
        247–55, 256, 258–59
Tonkin, Heather, 69
Transworld Publishers, 248
Trooping of the Colour, 82
Truman, Harry, 95
Turkey, 89–90

UKN, 256
University College Hospital, 28

Vale of the White Horse Hunt, 50
Vanezis, Peter, 228, 242–43
Veres, Laslo, 210
Versace, Gianni, 136, 139, 171
Vietnam War, 16
Villa Windsor, 167–68

Wallace, Anna, 22–23
Washington Post, 95
Wedding, 44–45, 47
Wells, Brenda, 199

Westminster Abbey, 269, 271–73
Wharfe, Ken, 73–74, 78–79, 88,
        92, 97, 99, 106, 107, 109,
        121
Wheeler, Peter, 232–33
Whittaker, James, 38, 55–56, 86
William, Prince of Wales, 27–28,
        50–51, 56, 80, 82, 83–84, 87,
        100, 116, 117, 122–24, 133,
        156, 159–61, 270
Williams, Rowan, Archbishop of
        Canterbury, 276
Wilson, A. N., 120
Windsor Castle, 39–40, 43, 98,
        123
Windsor Great Park, 133
Wingfield, Alexander "Kez,"
        168, 169–70, 173, 175–76,
        177, 179–80, 183–84,
        221–24
Worcester, Marquis of, 72

Yacoub, Magdi, 124
Yassin, Hussein, 149
Yassin, Joumana, 149